# KIDS OFF THE BLOCK

# KIDS OFF THE BLOCK

## THE INSPIRING TRUE STORY OF ONE WOMAN'S QUEST TO PROTECT CHICAGO'S MOST VULNERABLE YOUTH


DIANE LATIKER

WITH BETHANY MAUGER

BakerBooks

*a division of Baker Publishing Group*

Grand Rapids, Michigan

Published by Baker Books
a division of Baker Publishing Group
PO Box 6287, Grand Rapids, MI 49516-6287
www.bakerbooks.com

Printed in the United States of America



Library of Congress Cataloging-in-Publication Data
Names: Latiker, Diane, 1957– author. | Mauger, Bethany, author.
Title: Kids Off the Block : the inspiring true story of one woman's quest to protect Chicago's most vulnerable youth / Diane Latiker with Bethany Mauger.
Description: Grand Rapids, Michigan : Baker Books, [2020]
Identifiers: LCCN 2020004868 | ISBN 9781540900425 (paperback)
Subjects: LCSH: Latiker, Diane, 1957– | Kids Off the Block, Inc. | Poor youth—Services for—Illinois—Chicago. | Problem youth—Services for—Illinois—Chicago. | Community-based human services—Illinois—Chicago.
Classification: LCC HV1437.C4 .L38 2020 | DDC 362.7/756908110977311—dc23
LC record available at https://lccn.loc.gov/2020004868

ISBN 978-1-5409-0115-6 (hardcover)

Some names and details have been changed to protect the privacy of the individuals involved.

Published in association with Ambassador Literary Agency, Nashville, TN.

20 21 22 23 24 25 26 7 6 5 4 3 2 1

In keeping with biblical principles of creation stewardship, Baker Publishing Group advocates the responsible use of our natural resources. As a member of the Green Press Initiative, our company uses recycled paper when possible. The text paper of this book is composed in part of post-consumer waste.

This book is dedicated to all the young people
who believe they are alone, that no one cares,
and that society has disregarded them.
I believe in you, love you, and
will always be here if you need me.
You are everything!

# Contents

# Foreword

Diane Latiker is saving lives
Not just of future babies, husbands, and wives
But of children drowning now
In the downpouring rain
Of poverty, hopelessness,
Killings,
Abandonment, pain
Of shootings,
The absence of hugs,
Drugs,
Gangstering thugs
Mothers on meth death
Crack cocaine brains
Fathers on streets
Shouting blame games
Some have even forgotten their names
Some killed by police
Jailed, not released
Children lost and broken, cuffed tight
To the chair of don't nobody care about me

Despair
So, why should I care?
Why should I care?
Why should I care?
Diane Latiker's saving lives
Because she does care
And dares to risk all she holds dear
Never embracing
The dark cloud of fear
Not that she sometimes
Doesn't move past her tears
Not that she sometimes
Doesn't fall to her knees
And pray to God, please, please, please,
Show me the way
To get through another day
But she gets up
And spits in the face of despair
Cleans herself up
Fixes her hair
And opens her heart
To another young face
Looking for salvation
A safe hiding place
And she hugs them
Scolds them
Holds them and molds them
Till she sees them in peace
Then she opens her arms
Gives them release
Then guides them to look past their pains
Teaches them how to use their talents, their brains
To reach back to others

Teaches them what nobody really wants to hear
About the enemy within
Their fears, their fears, their fears
But Diane teaches to get in fear's face
Tell fear his butt is evicted
Get his butt up, out of your place
Pick up his doodoo,
'Cause you now need your sacred inner space
She teaches healing
To give yourself another chance
Stop choking on your vomit
Take off your chains of self-doubt
Take your stance, start your dance
Fear and self-doubt get out, get out!
Diane doesn't preach fantasy
She lives the price that has to be paid
She has piles of gravestones for those no longer here
And their voices scream at us from those stony bricks
They scream stop, stop, stop!
Stop falling for the tricks
Stop hating each other
And all that looks like you
Stop being the apple and not the tree
We know life's beating you to your hopeless knees
But if you don't stand up and see past your pains
You'll end up like us
Fear and anger
Turned into brick-like pus
We hope folks will hear
What Diane has to say
It's not about living just another day
It's not about just becoming another stone
But creating a future that you really own

Building your dreams out of what you learn and know
Get up, never stop, go, go, go
Diane's book
Is an inside look
At all she's had to live
Of all the challenges she's had to face
Diane is a hero to me
An example of all we could be
She's a gift that keeps giving
All she can give
Teaching by example
The life you can live
Because Diane Latiker is saving lives
Not just of future babies, husbands, and wives
But of children drowning now
In the downpouring rain
Of poverty, hopelessness,
Killings,
Abandonment, pain.

Bill Duke, actor, director, and producer

# Introduction

## HOW DID I GET HERE?

"Hey, Miss Diane, can we play?"

My eyes darted around the Curtis Elementary School gym, looking for the kid who called over the rubber thud of basketballs and squeaking shoes. There was Lamont, standing in the doorway with two of his boys. *What's he doing here?* I wondered.

"Hold on a minute, I'll be right back," I told the volunteer helping me wrangle the crowd. I walked past seventy-five kids running layup drills in their Kids Off the Block T-shirts and over to Lamont. "What's going on?" I asked him.

He held up his Jordans and nodded toward the court. "We wanna play."

I studied his face. I had known that boy for years, and not once had he shown up to the basketball program. He wouldn't even come to Kids Off the Block, the after-school program that I ran out of my home. I talked him into coming to the bowling alley with us once, but he never would set foot in my house.

"Miss Diane, I ain't sitting next to those *so-and-so's*," he told me then—only he didn't say *so-and-so's*. Too many rival gang members there, apparently.

I had no idea why he showed up that afternoon ready to shoot hoops. But I also knew I never turned anyone away who wanted to play.

"Cool, come on in." I pointed to the lines by each basketball hoop. "Go ahead, we just running drills now."

Lamont and his boys walked across the gym, their backpacks slung over their hoodies. I figured they'd change into their gym shoes and jump in with the other kids, so I turned my attention back to the program.

"Miss Diane, watch!" a boy hollered as he flung a basketball at the hoop.

I grinned and clapped, watching the ball sail toward the backboard and bounce into the net. "Nice shot!" I cheered. Three days a week, the gym a block from my house was filled with kids just dying to dribble and shoot. Basketball had a way of bringing boys together, no matter what block they came from or what gang they pledged their allegiance to.

Not fifteen minutes later, the door swung open and in walked TO.

*Oh, Lord*, I thought.

TO wasn't supposed to be there that day. Most days he showed up ready to play, but he had told me he couldn't come this time for one reason or another. And most days, I would have been thrilled to see him. But most days, Lamont wasn't there.

Everybody was scared of TO. The kids told me he still ran around with his gang, much as I fussed at him to quit. I couldn't go a day without somebody telling me about kids from TO's and Lamont's gangs shooting each other up. And now, members of both gangs were in the gym with seventy-five other kids.

"Oh, hey, TO!" I said nervously. I stood in front of him trying to steer him away from Lamont. *Lord, please don't let Lamont notice TO*, I prayed.

"Hey!" I whipped my head around at the sound. There was Lamont, glaring right at TO. *Too late.*

"I know that was you the other night!" he bellowed, charging toward TO with his boys behind him. TO didn't move, but he wasn't backing down. The look on his face said he was fixing to fight.

Both boys screamed at each other, hurling words that I never allowed my KOB kids to say in front of me. And there I was between them, in the middle of a screaming match.

"Calm down!" I tried to yell over them. "The other kids are watching. Stop!"

But they didn't. Before I could move, Lamont and his boys reached in their backpacks and pulled guns. Later, the other kids would tell me they were .45s, the kind of gun Dirty Harry carried. All I knew was they were huge. TO locked eyes with Lamont as two boys behind him whipped their guns out too.

Everything froze. From my peripheral vision, I could see the other kids staring, scared to move. No basketballs bounced now. There was just an eerie silence. I was nearly fifty years old, and I was stuck between a bunch of kids dead set on shooting each other. It was like something out of a movie, only in movies kids holding guns look scared, like they wouldn't actually shoot. Not these kids. Their faces were cold and hard. My heart pounded.

*If one of these boys gets killed up in here, I'll never forgive myself,* I thought. Images of their families flashed through my mind.

Something inside me snapped. How dare these boys ruin a perfectly good day of basketball? I was furious at them for putting all the lives in that gym at risk. If bullets started flying, any one of us could get hit. Not just the kids holding guns. Bullets don't care.

*No*, I thought. *Not today. I ain't letting this happen.*

I grabbed TO's collar, yanking him down to my height until our faces were just inches apart. If I could get through to him, everybody else would listen.

"TO, tell them to put the guns down!" I screamed. "Tell them! Put the guns down!"

"Miss Diane, I can't tell them to put the guns down!" he screamed right back at me.

"TO! We all gonna get shot! Tell them now! Tell them to put the guns down!"

"I can't, Miss Diane! I can't do it!"

Our voices grew louder and louder. My throat burned, but I kept screaming. No one tried to escape. The boys around me were so scared out of their minds, they couldn't move.

"TO!" I screeched. "Do it! Tell them to put the guns down!"

"I already told you I can't!"

"Tell them to put the guns down!"

My chest tightened, and I felt lightheaded as I tried to catch my breath. *Come on, TO*, I thought. *You better than this.*

Finally TO's shoulders dropped. "Put the guns down!" he commanded.

TO's boys lowered their guns and stared at Lamont. A split second later they took off running, busting through the gym doors and out onto the street, leaving TO in the gym.

Lamont and his guys were behind them with their guns in their hands.

I let go of TO's collar and hightailed it out of the gym and into the school. I raced down the hall as fast as I could to the principal's office. "Somebody give me the phone!" I cried out.

I could barely breathe as I called the police. I told them exactly where the boys were, and they contacted the police detective who happened to be in the neighborhood. All of them were caught right there in the street and taken to jail.

When I could finally breathe again, I stomped back to the gym. TO was still there, shuffling around with his hands in his pockets. I thought he might be apologetic. After all, his little dispute just about got all of us killed. But instead he glared at me.

"Miss Diane, what was he doing here?" he demanded, clearly referring to Lamont.

"You already know, TO," I said firmly. "I don't turn anyone away who wants to play. That's my rule."

He crossed his arms. "Well, then I'm not gonna come back."

"That's okay with me," I said. I knew he was bluffing anyway. "You can't tell me who I let come to my program. What you *are* gonna do is you're gonna stop bringing that mess with you."

"I didn't start it," he protested.

"No, that's right, you didn't. Lamont did. But you sure didn't stop it until I made you."

TO walked off in a huff. When he was gone, I closed my eyes and sighed. *Diane, what are you doing?* I thought. *What is wrong with you? You could've got yourself killed.*

This isn't how I'd envisioned spending my days after my kids were grown. I was supposed to be fishing and playing with my grandbabies. I was supposed to be free. Not once did

I think I'd spend every waking hour of freedom looking after somebody else's kids.

I didn't plan any of this. When I invited ten kids into my living room in 2003, I had no idea it would turn into a nonprofit that kept thousands of kids off the streets. I didn't know a bunch of teenagers would turn my life upside down, tear up my house, and threaten my marriage. I didn't know that I'd come to love them as my own, that I'd wake up every morning thinking about how I could help them that day, that I'd willingly step in front of guns for them. I didn't know I'd experience the joy of watching them not only survive but also leave gangs, graduate from high school, find good jobs. Or that I'd know all too well the heartbreak of seeing them fall back into old traps. Get caught up in the streets. Become more victims of gun violence.

None of this was my idea. And I certainly don't deserve the credit. I still don't understand why God chose me to do this. If I'd known what lay ahead, I probably would have said no. But He used me anyway.

And by His grace, I'm still here.

# "You Should Do Something with Those Kids"

The bell over the door jingled as my final client left. After hours of coloring hair, applying relaxers, and trimming split ends, I was beat, but my work still wasn't done. I picked up a broom and swept my station as my mom walked over from her booth and flopped down in my chair.

This had been our routine since the day she opened the beauty shop. I never wanted to be a hair stylist. I was working construction and loving every minute of it when my mom asked me to go to beauty school. She had always wanted to own a salon, but she wasn't going to do it without me and my five sisters. I was nearly forty years old—the last thing I wanted to do was go to school with a bunch of girls half my age. But I don't say no to my mom. Now, years later, here I was working in her salon.

"What you got going on this weekend?" she asked me.

"Oh, I don't know," I said absently, placing combs and scissors in the Barbicide jar sterilizer. "I think I might take Aisha and her friends somewhere. Maybe go fishing."

My youngest daughter, thirteen-year-old Aisha, was always running around with nine of her friends. They'd be outside all day running the streets, playing tag, and doing who knows what when school was out for the summer. I took them to ball games, swimming pools, or bowling alleys whenever I could—mostly to keep my eye on Aisha. I liked knowing what she was up to.

My mom looked at me and nodded seriously. "Yeah, you should do that. You should stay close to those kids."

I stopped wiping my counter. "Huh?"

"No, really," she said. "You should do something with those kids, Diane. They respect you."

"Ma, no they don't." I rolled my eyes. "You oughtta be with them. The whole time we're out somewhere, they be acting up. Even Aisha is acting up. All they do is complain when we go fishing: 'Miss Diane, this is so boring. Why you making us do this?'" I said, imitating that teenage whine.

My mom laughed. "Oh, I know they fuss at you. But they really do respect you. You should pay attention sometime."

"I already have, Ma. Those kids don't listen to me. They don't listen to nobody."

My tone said that was that, like her words hadn't weaseled their way into my brain. But my mom knew better. She raised her eyebrows at me as if to say, "Mm-hmm."

When Aisha and her friends ran in and out of my house the next day, I took a hard look at them. *What did Ma mean by all that?* I thought. *Why did she say, "Do something with those kids"? I already do plenty. What else is there?*

My mom pushed the barbecue into the backyard as I stood back watching Aisha. It was a beautiful July night, perfect for a cookout. We spent most summer nights sitting in the backyard with my husband, James, just talking and grilling burgers or chicken on the barbecue. But tonight I didn't have much to say. My mind was in a different place. I hoped that my mom wouldn't bring up yesterday's conversation.

"Did you think about what I said?" my mom asked.

I braced myself. *So much for not bringing it up.* "No, I didn't think about it," I said, avoiding her eyes. "But I will."

There was that look again, the same look as the day before.

"Okay then," she said slowly. "I hope you do."

I dumped charcoal into the barbecue and lit a match, grateful she didn't say anything else. *Why did she have to bring that up again?* I thought. *I don't have time to do anything else with these kids. I don't want to do this. Aisha's four years away from graduation. I'm supposed to be free, not running around with somebody else's kids.*

I hoped she would let it go this time, but I knew she wouldn't. She never lets anything go when she's serious. And for some reason she was serious about this.

Aisha's friends had been yelling, "Hey, Miss Diane!" while running in and out of my house since they were kids. We never said much beyond small talk, but Aisha filled me in on the basics. I knew more than a few of them were in gangs. Some of them were selling drugs. Some of them might have been using. *Ain't nothing I can do for those kids*, I thought. *They got bigger problems than I can handle.*

My mom always believed that my sisters and I could change the world—with or without any evidence to back that up. It didn't matter if we told her we were going to ride a cow down the middle of Michigan Avenue. She'd just say, "You ride that cow good because I know you can do it." Usually her belief gave me confidence but not this time. I knew how to take the kids fishing or to a show and send them home. That's it. *Ma's wrong*, I thought. *This is too much. I'm supposed to be fishing, not trying to fix these kids.*

The next day, my mom and I were in the backyard again. My aunt Pearl was there watering the backyard with a hose when my mom broke the silence.

"Pearl," she hollered over the noise of the hose. "You know, I told Diane she needed to do something with the kids."

Aunt Pearl nodded, a hand on her hip, the hose still spraying water. "You know what, I done thought the same thing. Diane's got a way with them kids. She really should do something."

I threw my hands in the air. *Here we go*, I thought. This was Mom's classic move. If I don't do what she wants, she gets everyone else in the family on her side until I have no choice.

"We all been talking about it," my mom said.

"Hold up, who's we?"

"Diane," my mom said, ignoring the question. "You need to do something. I know you know it too."

I didn't protest. I couldn't get the thought out of my head, even though I couldn't understand why. But I just couldn't say yes.

"Ma, I don't know what to do," I admitted.

"Well, just do something," she said. "Think about it."

I wasn't going to get away from this. These thoughts that kept running through my head, keeping me awake when I was supposed to be asleep, they were all from the Lord. He wanted me to do something. And He wouldn't let me off the hook.

I spent the next three days on my knees. *God, I don't want to do this*, I prayed. *I'm just a mom. I got problems with my own kids. I don't know what to do. I'm not a role model.*

I had my first baby when I was just sixteen. I married the guy, because that's what everyone said you're supposed to do. I was too young to know better. Ten years later, I was divorced with six kids. I didn't even have a high school diploma to help me. I had a few wild years after that. I thought God had forgotten about me, and I was tired of being the good girl—I wanted to know what it was like to be bad. I tried every drug and drink I could get my hands on and even had another baby in the process. But I still didn't feel satisfied. So I found myself at church again, asking Jesus to give me another chance. That's when I met James. He was loud and had more hair than I'd ever seen on a man—but he sure was cute. One wink and that was it for me. We were married two weeks later. I wouldn't recommend that to any of my daughters, but it worked for us. We had Aisha, we settled into Roseland, and life was good. But now I was forty-six. All but one of my kids were grown, and I was just a few years away from freedom. Hadn't the time for a new calling passed?

*God, please ask someone else to do whatever it is You're telling me to do*, I prayed. *If for some reason You really do want me to do this, give me a sign. I need some real proof that it's You before I jump. I need to know You're going to catch me.*

I didn't get a sign. But I also couldn't shake the feeling that this was His plan. On the third day—July 15, 2003—I stood at my front window watching Aisha and her friends playing and lifted up one last prayer. *God, what could I possibly do with them?*

And there it was. His answer: *Just listen, Diane*. I heard the words in my head clear as day. *Find out what they need. You'll know what to do.*

My eyes snapped open suddenly at the sound of Aisha's laughter. She and her friends were running all over the block playing tag. Most of them were thirteen or fourteen years old—not kids anymore but still not grown. I took a deep breath. *I'm going to go out there and ask them what they want to be when they grow up*, I thought. I'm not sure where that question had come from. These kids might laugh at me. But before I could stop myself, I had one foot in front of the other, out the door and down the front steps.

"Aisha!" I hollered. I waited for her to come running, but she didn't look at me. Those kids were carrying on so loud they couldn't hear me.

I tried again. "Aisha!"

She jerked her head in my direction. "What?"

"Y'all come over here a minute."

All ten of them shuffled over, forming a half circle around me. They stared, waiting for me to say something.

"What y'all think I'm fixing to do, make a speech?" I joked. I always make jokes when I'm nervous. Luckily, the kids didn't notice my motive and laid out laughing.

"Oooh, Miss Diane, you bad," said Senneca, one of Aisha's friends.

This was my chance. "I was just wondering, what do you guys want to be when you grow up?"

I barely finished my sentence before they all started interrupting each other, calling out at least five occupations each. They jumped up and down like five- and six-year-olds, carrying on like anything was possible. They wanted to be singers and rappers, teachers and lawyers, doctors and nurses. Aisha wanted to be a child psychologist, singer, therapist, and masseuse.

They hollered over one another until I held my hand up. "Wait a minute, wait a minute," I said, laughing. "Could you maybe choose just one?" *These kids still have dreams in them. These streets haven't taken that away.*

After they quieted down a minute, I spoke up again. "If I invited y'all into my house, would y'all come?"

They looked at one another, confused. "Miss Diane, we always come to your house," Aisha's friend Jamal said.

"No, I mean like come to my house, get off the street, that kind of thing," I stuttered.

But they all acted like they understood. "Yeah, Miss Diane, we'd come."

"Good, good." I tried not to smile too big. "I'm gonna get y'all off the block."

DaJuan, one of the boys, laughed. "Yeah, we gonna be the kids off the block."

We all froze. "That's it!" I cried. "You're the Kids Off the Block!"

I herded all ten of them into my living room. They flopped down on my sofas and chairs, barely fitting in that ten-by-twelve room. My mind was a complete blank. They all leaned forward in their seats, some of them drumming their fingers on the arms of my furniture. I couldn't tell if Aisha was confused or embarrassed.

*These kids think I'm fixing to do something big or amazing*, I thought. *But I have no clue what I'm even going to say.*

"Well," I said, "do y'all want to talk?"

They nodded halfheartedly.

"About what?" Jamal chimed in.

"I just want to know what's going on with y'all," I said.

Now they were confused again. "But Miss Diane, Aisha grew up with me!" a girl named Lisa said.

"Yeah," Richard chimed in. "You know my mom and dad. You know our people."

"Yeah, you know me!" a few others joined in.

The room buzzed as the kids talked over one another again. Aisha's loyalty to her mama overruled her embarrassment. "Hey!" she yelled. "My mom's talking!"

Everyone stared at their shoes, looking embarrassed.

"You right, I've heard some things," I said carefully. "But I want to hear from y'all what y'all are doing. What's going on at school? What's going on at home?"

For a few minutes we all sat in silence. Finally, I heard DaJuan's deep voice. "I'll go."

DaJuan had been following Aisha around like a little puppy for weeks. That boy thought the sun shined out of her toes or something. Now was his chance to impress her. I didn't know much about DaJuan, but I did know he was a talker. Catch him on the right subject and he could yak your ear off. Not only that, but this boy was big for his age and strong as a mule. None of the boys would play around boxing with DaJuan. DaJuan would knock them out cold. If I could get him to be vulnerable, I knew the rest would follow.

DaJuan looked down, avoiding eye contact with the other kids. "I guess most of y'all know my dad is locked up," he said, fidgeting with the couch cushion. "My mom, she's working at Burger King or Wendy's—one of those places over there. But she don't even make enough to keep the lights on. So . . ." DaJuan shrugged. "I got five brothers and sisters. I got to help."

He didn't tell us how he helped his mom but he didn't have to. Everybody knew he wasn't out flipping burgers or calling out orders. I'd seen him on the corner at night myself more times than I could count. Only one reason anybody stands on a Roseland street corner after dark. I fought to keep the words from bubbling out of my mouth. *Boy, you got to stop selling them drugs!* I thought. *You find another way to help your mama, but this ain't it!* But this was my time to listen.

"My mom needs help," DaJuan continued, his voice cracking. "But there's nobody. Ain't nobody gonna help us. I got to bring money home somehow. I don't want to do it that way. But nobody's giving me a real job. So I do what I gotta do. We gotta survive."

No one made a sound as DaJuan fought back tears. Jamal put his hand on DaJuan's shoulder, while Aisha and the girls sat next to him in support.

DaJuan finally took a deep breath. "I guess that's it. That's all I got."

"Thank you for sharing that," I said. Before I could ask if anyone wanted to go next, Jamal jumped in.

"Yeah, my dad ain't around either," Jamal said, trying his best to act like he didn't care. "Sometimes I see him. Most of the time I don't. We ain't got no money and no food. I gotta swipe food sometimes just to keep us going. We so hungry some nights I make my sisters ketchup and mayonnaise sandwiches."

The other kids laughed and pretended to gag. They thought he was making a joke but quickly stopped when they realized he wasn't.

"My mom don't care," he said. "Shoot, we don't even see her half the time either. She'll just up and disappear, not even telling us where she's going. Probably because my mom hates me."

"Jamal!" I shouted, but I stopped myself. *Don't you talk about your mama like that*, I thought. *No mama hates her child.* But I held my tongue.

Jamal just shook his head sadly. "No, Miss Diane. She tell me all the time."

My jaw dropped—I couldn't help it. I knew Jamal had a flair for the dramatic. Maybe this was one of his tall tales.

"You mean she gets mad sometimes? Yells at you?"

Jamal shrugged. "She says, 'I hate the day I had you.'"

No one knew how to take those awful words. The girls moved to Jamal now, patting his back even though they weren't so sure he was telling the truth.

He sighed. "I got to keep whiskey in my room just to survive in that house. That's the honest-to-God truth. It's the only way I can stay there."

I could nearly feel my heart break inside my chest as I watched him burst into tears.

"I think about it all the time—what did I do?" Jamal continued between sobs. "Why can't my own mom love me? Isn't that what moms are supposed to do?"

No one had ever heard Jamal share like that.

I was about to ask someone else to share when I heard Aisha pipe up. "I'll go," she said, looking at me pointedly. *Oh boy. I wonder what horror story this child is about to dredge up about me.*

Aisha's lip quivered as she began her tragic tale of being pulled out of her neighborhood elementary school to attend a well-respected Catholic school. I had to close my eyes to keep them from rolling into the back of my head. *Here we go*, I thought. *Throwing it in my face that I wanted my daughter to get a good education. Go complain about it to Oprah someday!*

I just knew the other kids would be on my side and back me up. But instead, as I looked around the room, I saw understanding nods.

"Yeah, I can see why you would be mad about that," one boy said.

By this point steam was pouring out of my ears. All these kids were turning me into the villain just for sending my kid to a better school. But I couldn't say a word. I had to listen to Aisha, just like I did to all the other kids.

One by one, the kids went around the circle sharing their stories. Hours passed and no one left, not even to get a snack or a glass of water. They stayed even when my husband burst through the door, hollering, "Hey! What are y'all doing in here?" They laughed for a minute at how loud he was, but they kept right on talking.

I didn't ask a single one of them to volunteer—they did it on their own. The only boy who didn't speak up when it was his turn was Isiah. But after everyone else had a chance to speak, Isiah took a deep breath.

"Y'all pick on me," he said calmly, making eye contact with each kid around the circle.

My eyes widened as I looked at each kid, horrified. I shot Aisha a look that made it very clear he better not be talking about her.

A few of them protested or laughed off his accusation. "Aw, nah, we don't pick on you," another boy said, trying to play it cool. Isiah would have none of it.

"Yes. You do," he said with the same steady tone. "Y'all think I'm dumb. But I'm not."

He turned to me. "I'm gonna be somebody great one day, Miss Diane. And they all gonna talk about me."

"Yes you are, Isiah," I said, choking back tears.

Suddenly I glanced at a clock—it was 8:30 p.m., more than four hours since they had first sat down in my living room.

"Oh, it's late!" I said, startled. "Everybody's got to go on home. It's getting dark."

I was interrupted by a chorus of protests. "It's summertime, Miss Diane!" Jamal said. "I ain't gotta be in till ten o'clock."

I shook my head. "We can talk more tomorrow. You all got to get home to your families."

When my living room was empty I collapsed on the couch. The long list of problems I'd just heard played through my head like a movie. *How am I going to get DaJuan off the street corner? What on earth am I going to do with what Jamal said? And when am I going to have a talk with Aisha?*

None of these kids looked perfect from the outside, but I had no idea how very grown-up their problems were. I was smack in the middle of an emergency, trying to save kids who had very urgent needs. Their problems were too big. Too big for me to handle anyway.

*Oh, Lord*, I prayed. *What in the world have I gotten myself into? What if I can't help them? I don't have super powers. I can't rush in and fix everything.*

In that quiet living room, I felt God speak. *You're right*, I sensed Him saying. *You can't. But you don't have to. Just trust Me.*

I did the only thing I could. I picked up my phone.

"Ma!" I cried. "You won't believe what these kids just said!"

# Can't These Kids Be Kids?

The next afternoon I sat back in a lawn chair on my front porch, fanning myself from the baking sun. My little brown brick, two-flat apartment turns into a sauna on hot days like that one. All summer long, my porch, with its wrought-iron columns, is my refuge. It was just past five that evening, but I struggled to keep my eyes open. If I'd slept a wink the night before, I couldn't remember it. Every time I tried to shut my eyes, I was back in my living room, surrounded by Aisha and her friends. Listening to their problems. Watching their faces as they unearthed their secrets.

These weren't kid problems. These were grown-people problems. These kids shouldn't be worrying about keeping bread in their pantries or whether somebody will shut off their lights or water the next day. They shouldn't have to wonder if their mama loves them, or whether they'll ever see their daddy again. They shouldn't feel like they'll get jumped on the way home from school if they don't join a gang. Yet these kids had laid out those problems with a shrug, as if they were a fact of life and there was nothing anybody could do.

*What can I do, Lord?* I prayed over and over. The night before, after I finally gave up on drifting off to sleep, I pulled out my itty-bitty laptop and stretched out on my bedroom floor, my face close to the screen. I waited, listening to the electronic whines and clicks as my laptop took its sweet time connecting to the slow-as-a-snail dial-up internet. Then I typed every phrase into Google that I could think of—*after-school programs, troubled teens, at-risk youth*—anything that might pull up some information that could help me. These kids needed more than a listening ear. They needed someone to help them change their lives. Sitting in my bedroom, as night slowly gave way to the light of dawn, I was clueless. I knew I was on a mission from God, but I felt like He forgot to give me the instruction manual.

Now I closed my eyes as I leaned back in my lawn chair. My feet swelled in my gym shoes and my back ached after a long day behind my salon chair. A job I'd never enjoyed had felt particularly unbearable that day. I had tuned out my clients as they droned on and on, only throwing in a "Mm-hmm" or "Really?" here and there. I was too busy thinking about how to get DaJuan to stop selling drugs. My shoulders sank with relief when my mom flipped around the CLOSED sign on the door.

*I need you, Lord*, I prayed. *You gotta help me help these kids.*

The scream of a siren jerked me out of my prayer. I sat up a little straighter, scanning Michigan Avenue. *That's the police*, I thought. I'd heard enough sirens to know whether a police car, ambulance, or fire engine was heading my way. Sirens are just a part of life when you live in Roseland.

I remember visiting my auntie on the South Side in Roseland when I was a kid and thinking I'd never seen a more beautiful neighborhood. Mama would load us into the car and hop on the expressway, taking I-94 all the way down. The drive from our home on the west side took less than half an hour, but I could have sworn we were in another city. I took in the manicured lawns with daisies and marigolds lining flower beds. The blocks were booming with crowds at movie theaters and bowling alleys and men and women filling the corner diners and lounges. Even the people seemed friendlier, smiling from their porches and waving at everybody who passed. Dutch and Irish families lived there alongside black folks like my auntie.

"One day, I'm gonna get me a house down here," I told my mom.

But by the time James and I moved into my mom's apartment building in 1988, Roseland had already begun its steady decline. The steel mill that once provided steady paychecks for the neighborhood's families boarded up its windows, and the Pullman company scaled back on its famous railroad cars. And as black families like mine moved in, white families fled like their hair was on fire. Back when my auntie lived in Roseland, the neighborhood was about 20 percent black. Just a few decades later, if you saw a white face, you just knew they were from out of town.

When the white people left, businesses left right along with them. Abandoned buildings lined the streets, boarded-up windows more plentiful than glass ones. The only businesses that dared to stay were liquor stores, gas stations, and a barber shop here and there. They hunkered down like they were in a war zone, protecting their windows with bars and locking up their bottled water and candy bars under Plexiglas. Clerks worked behind bulletproof plastic. Cameras mounted on lampposts recorded every move on the streets. Burned-out houses were left to rot. Buildings were marked with an *X* but never torn down. Shiny new shopping centers and pristine city streets were just miles away, but we were stuck living in an endless battle. My home, the place where I'd dreamed of living, was written off by the powers that be. I'd be lying if I said I didn't feel forgotten. No one cared about Roseland anymore.

Young people had no movie theater or bowling alley where they could pass the time. They had no hope that they'd grow up to get a good job, buy a house, and provide for their families without worrying about how they'd put food on the table. All that was left for them was the street corner. That's when the violence came.

Chicago had always been home to gangs, but there was a limit to what they would do. I grew up understanding that women and children weren't targets. But that wasn't true anymore. As the years went by, anyone who found themselves in the wrong place at the wrong time could get caught in the crosshairs. Mamas stopped letting their babies play outside. Playgrounds sat eerily quiet. Every day brought another gunshot in the distance, another cross adorned with flowers on the sidewalk, another life cut short. That's why these kids joined gangs. They felt they had to if they wanted to walk to school or to the corner gas station safely.

This was my home. I was aware of every sound, every movement, every person who didn't belong. I'd learned how to stop being scared all the time. Nobody was going to force me to sit in my house all day. But I wasn't stupid. I'd seen too many drive-bys to think it couldn't happen again on my block.

*That's why these kids can't even be kids*, I thought. *What kind of childhood can you have when you always looking over your shoulder?*

"Hey, Miss Diane!"

I looked up to see Brittany on the front lawn. I smiled and waved before I hollered for Aisha to come out of the house. Brittany lived next door, and she and Aisha were always carrying on together. Lord knew those two had enough personality for ten girls and an opinion about everything, but they got along like sisters.

The usual group of kids ended up in front of my house before long. My mom joined me on the front porch. I hadn't told the kids to come back in my house the next day, but as their game of tag died down, they all slowly made their way over to the porch.

"Hey, Miss Diane. Hey, Miss Jackson," they greeted us.

I looked around at the ten boys and girls crowding onto my little porch, leaning against the railing. Jamal looked back at me with his big brown eyes, his face creased with worry. I knew he was wondering if I'd told anybody about what he'd said the night before.

Suddenly an idea hit me. "Ma, you got your anointing oil with you?" I didn't really have to ask. I knew she always had some in her purse or pocket. My mom stood up and pulled out a little bottle. "Can you pray for all them?" I asked her.

Not one kid protested as my mom carefully smeared oil on each of their foreheads. They closed their eyes and stretched their arms to the sky as my mom and I laid our hands on them and prayed. My mom cried out to the Lord for each and every one of them by name. If anyone didn't want to pray, they didn't dare say so. They knew better than that. The Spirit was there with us on that porch. I could feel it.

When we finally opened our eyes, I stood up to head inside and start fixing dinner. Without saying a word, those kids shuffled right across my porch, following me to my door.

"Where y'all going?" I asked. The kids looked at one another before Jamal spoke up.

"Ain't you gonna talk to us again tonight?" Jamal asked.

I stared at him. I knew I couldn't tell him no. "Well, I can if y'all want me to."

"We want you to!" they said. Before I could say another word, they all filed into my house.

The boys flopped down on my sofa and flung their Jordans on my wood coffee table. I resisted the urge to yell at them to get their feet off my furniture. Now wasn't the time. Not when they were relaxed for the first time all day. In my living room, nobody was worried about the gangs coming after them or whether there was enough food in their cupboards back home. The boys laid out laughing as they went back and forth doing the dozens: one kid would make a joke about another kid, and the other would go right back at him. Jamal was always in the middle of it.

"DaJuan, you need to wash them gym shoes!" he yelled. "Smell like roadkill up in here."

But DaJuan didn't get mad. This was just part of the dozens. He was used to it. "Shut up with that lump on your head, lump man!" he shot back.

Jamal was speechless for a moment. Everybody knew he actually did have a lump on his head. He had to wear his hair just right so it wouldn't show. DaJuan looked satisfied.

"Fa-wow!" he said as Aisha and the girls cracked up. That's what all the kids said when they made a joke that got a big laugh. I don't even know what it meant, but they said it every time. I felt a little bad laughing about Jamal's lump, but their laughter was contagious.

Between jokes, the kids poured out stories about their day like they'd been bottled up.

"Miss Diane, I did what you said about those girls who been talking about me!" Senneca piped up. "And you know what, you were right! They done left me alone after that."

It was all I could do not to fall out of my seat. I gave a little bit of advice the night before, but I never really thought anyone would pay attention. And yet here was Senneca, doing exactly what I said. Maybe my mama was right. Maybe these kids really did listen to me.

Those kids barely left my living room the whole night, aside from one or two who needed to check in with their mamas here and there. I never knew how late it was. I wasn't worried about organizing activities for them or anything like that just yet. All I wanted was to get to know them better, feel them out. Every once in a while, James would creak down the hall, scratching his head and squinting in the light.

"Y'all need to quiet down!" he hollered. "I got to go to work tomorrow!"

"We'll be quiet," I assured him, even though I was the loudest one of all. Something was happening to me. The aches and pains I'd felt since the day I turned forty disappeared in those hours. I stopped feeling too tired to get off the couch after work. Days that once stretched on and on now seemed full of possibilities. I was more excited than the kids in my living room.

So I didn't make them go home. I didn't care that I, too, had to be up for work the next day. I stayed up with them way past midnight and even made up my couches and living room floor with pillows and blankets for anyone who wanted to spend the night.

I didn't know what I had started. All I knew was that I was filled with an energy I had never experienced. All week long, I'd force my feet to carry me downstairs to my mom's basement salon when I'd rather be carrying on with the kids. Physically, I was there relaxing my clients' hair and answering "yeah" in all the right places, but in my head, I was busy thinking of what I could do with the kids that night. As soon as I walked outside, the kids would be standing by the salon door waiting for me. "You hangin' out with us, Miss Diane?" they'd ask. Then we'd head back to my house for KOB—that's what we called Kids Off the Block.

We'd go upstairs and do it all over again. Every night was filled with laughter and doing the dozens and standing on the porch, keeping an eye on kids walking down the street to the gas station at three or four in the morning because somebody wanted chips or a pop. They were in and out of the house at all hours, asking me for fifty cents and running back and forth between my house and theirs or the gas station—I always watched them to make sure they were safe. I could see the station from my porch. We'd hush when James hollered at us, but one joke from DaJuan was enough to send us all laughing so hard I had to run to the bathroom so I didn't pee my pants. These boys were the size of grown men, and they flopped on my sofas so many times that the legs were about to give out, the cushions ripped, the middle sagging. All my furniture looked like it had aged about ten years in a week. I should have been exhausted. But I felt fresh. Exhilarated. Ready to take on the world.

By the end of the week, I knew it was time to get these kids doing something productive. I hatched a plot late at night, when the last kid had finally passed out. We couldn't stay up all night talking and laughing forever. God wanted me to do something more. And after a few more nights of praying, I started to get a feel for what that might be.

The group didn't know what was coming when they burst through my screen door and found a spot on the floor—the couch was already gone. I'd had the boys help me carry it out to a dumpster.

"Oooh, listen, I got a song I want y'all to sing," I said when they'd all sat down.

The room erupted with protests. "Aw, nah, Miss Diane, we ain't no singers," DaJuan said.

The girls rolled their eyes as Aisha said, "Here we go again."

"No, no, come on!" I pulled out my little tape player and popped in a cassette. "It's gonna be fun. I want y'all to learn this Luther Vandross song, 'Take You Out.'"

The protests grew to a roar. "My mama listens to that, not me!" Isiah held up his hands and shook his head.

I ignored them and turned on the song. I nodded and swayed along with the beat, trying to get the kids into it. They weren't having it.

"Miss Diane, that's a punk song." Jamal pushed his bottom lip out and rolled his eyes. "I ain't singing that."

I pulled out my ink pen and pricked him in the arm playfully—that's what I always did with the kids when they tried to bump their chest at me and say something smart. "Jamal, hush. Ain't nobody talking to you."

When the song ended, I handed each boy a sheet I'd printed out the night before with the lyrics on it. "Now I want y'all to learn this. I got a part for each of you. We'll work on the song here, and y'all can sing together like a group."

All ten of them looked at me, highly disappointed. I sucked in my breath, trying not to laugh at their aggrieved expressions.

"You make us sing this, I'ma call the people on you, call DHS." Jamal crossed his arms and shook his head. "'Cause this here is child abuse."

I reached for my cordless. "Do you want the phone?"

Jamal grumbled as he grabbed his song-lyric sheet. I raised my eyebrows at him and nodded as if to say, "Yeah, that's what I thought."

We listened to the song a few more times before I asked if anyone wanted to try singing first. Everybody's jaws dropped when DaJuan raised his hand. "I'll go."

DaJuan stood up in the living room, the rest of us on the floor staring up at him. He looked down at his feet as he opened his mouth to sing. No one moved as he croaked out the first few lines of the song. I forced my mouth into an encouraging smile, trying not to grimace. Bless that boy's heart, he couldn't sing a lick. I don't know what notes he was singing, but they sure didn't sound anything like the song I'd just played.

"Alright, alright, sit down." Jamal stood up and adjusted his jeans like he was about to show us how it was done. "Let me try."

Jamal popped his hip and curled his lips like he was Rico Suave. The music coming out of his mouth did not match his attitude. The girls and I laughed so hard we got the hiccups.

One by one, the boys each took a turn giving the song their best shot. Richard sang so quietly nobody could even hear him. A few boys tried to rap the lyrics instead of singing. Isiah was the only one to impress us, his deep voice echoing through the room.

Finally, I looked over at the girls, who'd spent the last hour sitting back laughing. "Don't you think you're off the hook," I said, pulling out another stack of paper. "I got something for you too."

Suddenly, they weren't laughing anymore. All three of them turned to me, eyeing me suspiciously. "What is it?" Aisha asked.

I didn't say a word as I handed them the lyrics to "C'Mon, Young People." This wasn't a song they'd heard anywhere else. This song was mine.

Most of my life, I'd kept a ratty old spiral notebook, where I wrote poems and songs. Back in the day, my sisters and I even had an R&B singing group. I wasn't much of a singer, but I loved writing our songs.

Since these kids had come into my life, words just poured out of me. I'd lie awake at night, thinking of what Jamal's mom had said to him the day before or how scared Lee was to walk down the street, and I'd burst out crying. When no one was in my salon chair, I pulled out a pen and started writing. I wanted to write something that would inspire young people to do something positive for themselves. I wanted them to know they could be responsible. If they refused to be victims of their circumstances, if they stood up and took control, their lives could change.

I knew as soon as I was finished that the poem needed to be a song. Luckily, my brother-in-law just happened to be a music producer. I called him up the next day and asked him to put the song to music.

That evening in my living room, the girls were quiet as I switched on the track he'd sampled from Gladys Knight and the Pips' song "If I Were Your Woman." Without an explanation, I sang my lyrics for them.

> Telling parents to leave us alone
> Thinking we are so grown
> They are out there trying to survive
> They need us in their lives
> Hurting everybody
> Thinking we're somebody
> Wake up, get up
> Be different
> C'mon, young people
> Let's get it together
> This is our situation
> We're killing each other

No one said a word as they listened. And let me tell you, these girls are never quiet. I knew that meant they liked it.

"Let's listen to that again," Brittany said when the track ended. We listened again. And again. The girls chattered about who could sing which part and what harmonies they should sing for the chorus. I felt my chest swell with pride as they buzzed with excitement about a song I'd written.

They went on like that the rest of the evening—the girls in the dining room, the boys in the living room. Every once in a while, James would slide through, crooning along with them. He'd fussed at us since the first day these kids showed up, but he wasn't fussing this time. Singing was right up his alley. I always say I married the black Elvis. The girls were careful not to let the boys hear them until they had their song down. They were too concerned with looking cute in front of the boys to risk hitting a wrong note.

*I think I'll invite their families to come watch*, I thought. *Show them what we've been doing*. But I forced myself to stop the constant flow of ideas that swirled through my head. I stopped making plans. I stopped scheming. I leaned against the plaster wall next to my burgundy curtains, watching the kids with a smile. Nobody was thinking about their problems. They weren't worried about the gangs prowling outside. In this moment, they were kids acting like kids. Exactly as it should be. My living room had become a safe haven. Their sanctuary. *Lord, even if that's all I do, I know that's a success*, I prayed. *Help me let these kids be kids.*

## CHAPTER THREE

# "Are You Miss Diane?"

Corey showed up in my living room without so much as a knock on the door just a week after I first invited those ten kids inside. I never thought it would go beyond those ten. I figured I would hang out with Aisha and her friends, mentor them as best I could, and help them stay off the streets. But my door was always open, and Corey walked right in.

I took in the tall, heavyset boy looking around like he owned the place. "Hello," I called out to him. "And who are you?"

"I'm Corey," he said. "I went to school with Aisha over at Curtis. I know Jamal and them. I been around."

"Okay, make yourself comfortable."

I was about to introduce him when Jamal and the other kids noticed him.

"Oh, Lord have mercy," Jamal scoffed. The boys laughed as I looked at them, confused.

"This dude right here," Jamal said, pointing to Corey. "He don't know when to quit. He always raggin' on us."

"Yeah, but he can sing," Aisha chimed in.

"Oooh, yeah, you gotta hear him, Miss Diane," Senneca said.

Corey nodded as the other kids made commentary. I could see he wasn't the modest type.

"That true?" I asked him. He nodded. "Sing me something right now."

That caught him off guard. "Right now?"

"Right now."

When I tell you this boy knocked my socks off, I am not exaggerating. You would have thought Ruben Studdard was standing in front of us. I can't remember the song Corey sang, but the voice coming out of his mouth was unlike anything I'd ever heard in person.

I could barely speak when he was finished. I couldn't find a compliment that would come anywhere close to the beauty of the music I'd just heard. All I could say was, "Welcome to KOB."

Corey jumped into our little group like he'd been there since day one. He took the lead on that Luther Vandross song the boys had worked on for days and made it actually sound like music. He told stories right along with the rest of the kids and stayed at my house late into the night. But it wasn't long before I understood why Jamal and the kids had reacted the way they did when they saw him in my house. That boy had a mouth on him unlike anybody I'd ever seen. Morning and night, he talked smack about anybody and everybody—including me. He'd laugh and say he was just doing the dozens, but he always took it one step past funny. But if you had the nerve to say something about him, look out. He could dish it out, but he sure couldn't take it.

I didn't take his words personally. I figured he was insccure about being heavyset, and he defended himself with insults. The other kids didn't see it that way. Corey's words made everyone hot under the collar. Especially Jamal. One night, Jamal jumped on his feet after Corey included a few choice words about Jamal's mama.

"You say one more thing, I'm gonna take you outside," he sputtered.

I can't remember exactly what Corey said, but I knew it wasn't right. Even Aisha and Brittany spoke up, telling Corey to back off. He laughed.

"I'm just telling the truth," he said, shaking his head.

"Alright then." Jamal hitched up his pants and sniffed. "Let's go outside."

I glanced at the clock. It was 3:30 in the morning.

"Yeah, you know what, let's go outside," I said. The kids stared at me, shocked. *If these boys want me to stop them, I ain't gonna give them the satisfaction*, I thought. "Let's go. I'ma watch y'all beat each other's brains out."

The whole group shuffled nervously out of the house. I herded them out to the front yard and stood back, my arms crossed. I raised my eyebrows as if to say, "Alright then, go ahead."

Jamal and Corey faced each other, their chests puffed out as they picked up their argument right where they'd left off. The rest of the kids waited on the porch. Would one of these boys really take a swing at the other?

Minutes ticked by. Nobody moved. They were afraid to fight. At the same time, nobody wanted to be the one to back down. So instead, they just kept yelling.

Finally, I couldn't take it anymore. "Neither one of y'all are gonna bust a grape," I said as I put my hands on their shoulders. "Let's go."

It wasn't the last time they argued, but they stopped threatening to beat each other.

The next morning I yawned as I sat down to breakfast with James. I wasn't sure what time I'd finally climbed into bed and closed my eyes, but I knew it was way too late. James had rolled over angrily as I told him good night. Not that I blamed him. Nobody likes to be woken up in the middle of the night. I'd hoped a few more hours of sleep would be enough to cool him off, but as he grunted in response to my "Good morning," I knew he wasn't over it.

I kept trying to make conversation with him. I should have backed off and shut my mouth, but I hated the thought of him being mad at me. After one too many questions, James put his coffee cup down and sighed.

"Diane, what are you doing?" His voice was tense.

I shrugged. "I don't know."

"No, you know." James shook his head and held out his hands. "You're up all hours of the night with these kids. They're in here destroying our stuff, keeping me up, being loud. And I don't like it."

James was calm—almost too calm. Maybe his words would have been easier to take if he was yelling. Maybe then I could have written them off. But I could tell he meant them. And deep down, I knew he had a point.

"You're right." I couldn't argue. "I'm trying to help these kids, and I don't know what I'm doing. But can you just bear with me? At least until I figure this out."

"Help these kids? We can't help these kids." Now James's voice grew louder. "We can barely help ourselves."

Tears stung my eyes, much as I tried to stop them.

James leaned forward and looked deep into my eyes. "We can't live like this, Diane. We can't have these kids keeping us up when we gotta work the next day. I'm tired of this. And you ain't gonna be able to keep this up." He took a deep breath and paused before turning away from me. "You gonna have to let these kids go."

"I can't." I could barely get the words out as my throat choked back sobs. "This is something I have to do. I can't explain it. I just know God gave this to me."

James stood up. "You didn't even ask me. You're gonna turn our whole life upside down and not even talk to me first?"

He was right. Right about everything. But it was too late to turn back now. And I needed him. Those kids lit up when he walked into the room. I dreamed of him standing by my side, mentoring them right along with me. I wanted him to tell me I was doing the right thing, that I could help them, that I had what it took. I didn't need this fight.

"I just wish you would support me," I finally said.

Any hope of solving this problem disappeared as James pushed back his chair and stormed off. I watched him tie his shoes and grab his work bag. The whole house rattled as he slammed the door behind him to leave for work.

It wasn't our first argument about KOB. And it sure wasn't a secret that he wasn't exactly thrilled about the kids crowding our house. Most nights he hollered at us at least once to pipe down, and he made a big show of how tired he was the morning after we were especially loud, yawning and rubbing his eyes like he was auditioning for a sleeping pill commercial. But this was the first time he'd confronted me about it.

I knew I should have talked to him. I should have made sure he was okay with it before I let these kids take over our living room, destroy our furniture, raid our refrigerator. But at the same time, what would I have said? I had no idea these kids would come back day after day, following me from the salon to the house and staying all night long.

*James will calm down*, I told myself. *As long as it's just these kids, he'll be alright. He'll get used to them. He might even learn to love them too. It's only eleven kids.*

"Aisha, who is that?"

We were all out front picking up trash and sweeping up the block. By now, we were four weeks into Kids Off the Block, and I wanted these kids to spend some of their time doing something useful. So I hauled out a bunch of shovels and rakes and put them to work sweeping up trash, leaves, and sticks.

I was busy sweeping the sidewalk when I noticed a tall boy I didn't recognize talking to Jamal and DaJuan. I figured he must be somebody from Aisha's little group.

But Aisha shrugged. "I don't know. I ain't ever seen him."

I frowned. That was strange. I moved in a little closer so I could hear what he was saying.

"Yeah, I'm from over there on Perry," I heard him say. "But my brother went to Curtis. He knows somebody who told me about y'all." He listed off a few names he thought the other boys might recognize, trying to make himself known, like he was just six degrees of separation from them.

DaJuan's face flickered with recognition. "Oh, you one of them Harris boys." The boy nodded. Before I knew it, he was picking up a rake and working alongside the rest of the group, laughing and carrying on like he'd known them his whole life.

When it was time to go in the house, this new boy shuffled in with everyone else. He plunked down in one of the folding chairs I'd set up in my living room and kicked his feet up, blending right in with the group.

"And who might you be?" I asked him when everybody sat down.

"I'm Cole," he said. He was a cute boy, with smooth, dark skin and a smile so big he looked like he had extra teeth. From the way Aisha was looking at him, I knew I wasn't the only one who'd taken notice of his appearance. I gave her the side-eye. *You better watch yourself.*

"And what do you like to do, Cole?"

There was that too-many-teeth smile again. "I'm a basketball superstar."

I couldn't help but smile back. "Oh, you think you got skills? Wait till I get that ball."

The whole room cracked up. Everybody knew I could barely dribble. But this was my way of tearing down his walls.

"What brought you over here?" I asked him.

"I heard some kids talking about y'all," he said. *Who does this kid know who's talking about us?* I sure hadn't been out hanging up flyers or spreading the word.

"So you just took a chance to come around here then?"

"Yeah." He nodded. "You Miss Diane, right?"

Now how did he know that? But I just nodded back. "Yeah, I'm Miss Diane."

Cole melded into the group, talking to the boys and smiling at the girls while Aisha and Jessie made goo-goo eyes at him. *If this kid has already heard about us, who else has?* I wondered. *Is somebody else going to show up too?*

I wouldn't have to wonder long. Within a few days, another stranger opened my screen door and made himself at home.

"Now, who are you?" I asked him.

"I'm CJ," he announced. "I'm Cole's cousin."

*Okay, thirteen kids,* I thought. *James shouldn't fuss too much over thirteen. We'll just keep it at that.*

But then Rico showed up. Rico was a mature, laid-back fifteen-year-old who had heard we were a full-fledged organization with programs and everything. If he was disappointed, he didn't let on.

"I'm gonna tell the other boys to come too," he told me. Who those boys were, I had no idea. I figured it might be a handful of kids. I didn't know the floodgates were about to open.

Rico was something of a leader over on State Street. All the other boys wanted to be like him. So when he came to KOB, everybody followed. After Rico came Quincy. And Elliott. And Mason. Parker. Warren. Stanley and his brother. Every time I turned around, another kid I didn't recognize was standing in front of me, asking, "Are you Miss Diane?"

Then came the girls. They all wondered where the boys had disappeared to, so they crowded into my little house too.

As more kids showed up, I saw more scowls and crossed arms from my original ten. They watched me like a hawk every time I had a one-on-one conversation with Cole or cut up with Rico and the new guys. Especially Jamal. Jamal was like a little boy jealous of a new sibling.

"Miss Diane, I've seen these kids," he'd whisper loudly. "Cole hangs around some bad kids. And he did—"

"He did what, Jamal?" I crossed my arms and gave him a firm look. I knew what his real problem was. I knew he liked Aisha, and he wasn't too keen on Cole cozying up to her.

"It ain't just him!" he protested. "I don't trust Rico and them. They over there running State Street. Something ain't right."

"Jamal, those boys ain't nothing more than ballers. They ain't even in a gang."

But Jamal just shook his head. "I don't like them, Miss Diane. They bad."

I sighed. I was in no mood to play referee between Jamal and the boys moving into his territory. I was already scrambling to figure out what on earth to do with these kids who had already filled my house to bursting.

From my front window I could see the vacant lot across the street. I'd never cared much for it. A vacant lot was just a place for gangs to fight and cause trouble. But now that more than thirty kids regularly crowded into my house, I looked at that gray asphalt with new eyes.

You couldn't turn around in my house without finding a kid hanging on the Formica kitchen counter, lounging in a folding chair, or sitting crisscross on the living room floor. The air was thick with a mix of sweat, gym shoes, and cheap cologne. You could smell it even when the house was empty. I braced myself against James's fussing as I turned our tiny spare bedroom into a music studio just so we could breathe a little.

Every night, I had kids rapping in the spare room, singing in the living room, and huddling together on the porch in hushed conversations. The music of Destiny's Child and Keri Hilson thumped through the house as the girls choreographed intricate moves and practiced their steps in the dining room. I floated from room to room, making sure the boys kept their rap lyrics clean and the girls didn't shake a little too much booty.

Someone was always tugging at my arm. "Miss Diane, can I talk to you?" they'd ask. I always said yes. They'd tell me about how they got a letter from their father they hadn't seen in years or how they got into it with their mom earlier that morning. Girls would whisper, "Miss Diane, sometimes my stomach hurts real low. What can I take?" Every day it was something. No matter what it was, I treated each kid and each problem with equal importance. "Let's step to the side," I'd say as I listened and dished out advice.

I should have been exhausted. But every morning, I woke up excited for the day to come. All I had to do was make it through a few hours of doing hair before I could meet the kids outside and get back to KOB. My whole life, I'd never had a passion outside of caring for my family. Whether I was hammering nails on a construction crew or pouring drinks at a lounge, all I'd ever done during daytime hours was work for a paycheck. I'd go home to a quiet house, fix dinner, and fuss at James to pick up his shoes or Aisha to finish her homework. We'd watch TV for a few hours before passing out in bed. I'd wake up the next day to do it all again.

Now I felt awake for the first time in years. I had a passion. I had a purpose. My life meant more than just making enough money to get by. I was helping these kids. I could see it in the way they trusted me and the way they told me about the different choices they made when they weren't in my house. I couldn't get enough of this new life.

But we needed more room. By now, the sixty sneakered feet that tracked through my dining room each day had worn my thick red carpet down to the floorboards. We ended up ripping it out. I gave up on furniture except for James's La-Z-Boy recliner and big-screen TV. I set up a few folding chairs and rolling computer chairs. The vacant lot looked more attractive with every day that went by. *Maybe we could do something over there*, I thought.

I could barely keep the kids away from the car as James helped me lug a giant box out of the back seat one day.

"Miss Diane, what is that?" they hollered. "What you got?"

When they saw the picture on the front, they just about lost their minds. James and I had just come back from a trip to Sport Mart. I'd paid fifty-nine dollars plus tax for a little rolling basketball hoop we could drag over to the vacant lot.

"Well, don't just stand there," I said. "Help me put this thing together."

The boys grinned and jabbered as they screwed bolts into place, ribbing at one another the whole time. "Man, I can't wait to get this over there," they'd say. "You better look out, 'cause I'm gonna dribble on you so hard."

From then on, as long as it wasn't freezing or raining, we hauled that basketball hoop across the street. These hardened teenage boys giggled like kids as they played knockout, three-shot, or three-on-three games. Most of the boys in KOB loved basketball almost as much as they loved showing off. I couldn't get up to go to the bathroom without somebody yelling, "Wait a minute, Miss Diane! Watch this! I'ma make this shot!" And if I turned to walk to the gas station for more juice and water, I'd hear somebody holler, "Miss Diane's going to the store!" Before I knew it, thirty kids were following me.

Anybody who wasn't shooting or passing the basketball sat on the sidelines, cheering on the other kids. I sat with them in my folding chair, handing out sandwiches and chips or talking to the kids who didn't want to play.

Every day, somebody else would show up on the lot in their shorts and gym shoes. "Can I play?" they'd ask. I never turned anybody down. I just explained I had two rules: no fighting and no cursing—especially not the N-word. When I folded up the chairs and rolled the hoop back to the house, I always had a few more kids with me than when I started.

By the end of three months, I knew we needed more structure. I got a little savvier after reading about after-school programs online. Everything I read said I needed to keep track of who was coming. So I set out two spiral notebooks and made the kids sign in when they walked through my door each day. I never expected to see seventy-five names scrawled on a day's sign-in sheet, but one evening, there they were.

*Seventy-five?* My mind raced. *How on earth did this happen? How did I go from ten kids in my living room to seventy-five?*

James was less than thrilled. Every day was a battle: somebody ate his sandwich or somebody sat in his chair, like he was Baby Bear, forced to live with Goldilocks.

"What are you doing, Diane?" he grumbled at me. "Why are you doing this? You can't keep this up. You can't handle this many kids."

All I could say was, "I don't know." I couldn't handle it. Sometimes I wondered if I should just give in, quit now, walk away.

But every time I thought about quitting, something would happen. The Lord would remind me why He put me here in the first place. Like the day Jamal's mom marched into my house. Jamal and I were in the dining room while the other kids were on the front porch. The other kids must have told her we were inside. I'd seen Jamal's mom from time to time, but we'd never had much of a conversation.

"Hi," I called out to her. "How are you?"

She didn't answer. She just walked straight toward Jamal, her hand on her hip.

"Jamal, why ain't you been doing your chores at the house?" she demanded.

Jamal never seemed smaller than he did in that moment. He shrank back in his chair like he was a little kid. "I ain't been there," he said carefully. "I was over here with Miss Diane."

"I don't care where you were," she hissed. "You don't never listen." She wrinkled her nose like she'd smelled something awful. "That's why I hate that you was born."

I froze. I'd heard Jamal talk about his mama and how she hated him, but I never believed any mother could truly feel that way about her child. Now that I'd witnessed it with my own eyes, I was speechless.

Jamal turned to me, tears brimming in his big eyes. I felt myself melt into the floor as I stared back at him. *I'm sorry*, I tried to say with my eyes. *You don't deserve this*.

If his mama saw how she'd hurt him, she didn't care. She walked out of the house without another word.

As soon as we heard the door slam shut, Jamal collapsed into my arms. I felt his chest heave with sobs, his tears soak through my T-shirt. All I could do was hold him.

"Shhh," I whispered, stroking his hair and wiping his tears. "You gonna be okay. It's okay."

This boy needs me, I realized. All of these kids do. Whether I knew what I was doing or not, I couldn't walk away.

# Resistance from Every Side

It started with a knock on the front door.

I opened it to find police officers, hats perched on their heads, their arms crossed. *Oh, Lord, what are they doing here?* I thought. *Was our music really that loud?*

"Is everything alright here?" one of the officers said.

I nodded as politely as I could. "Yes, sir," I said. "We fine." They barely said another word before they turned to leave.

*Now what was that about?* I wondered. You don't see the police in my neighborhood unless there's some kind of problem. I've never been shy about calling the police. I know a lot of folks around Roseland would rather take care of their own business. The kids say, "Snitches get stitches." Our community's relationship with the police has always been complicated. But as for me, I don't play. I will call the police in a heartbeat, and I make sure the kids in my program understand that too.

Still, I'd be lying if I said my heart didn't pound a little faster when I opened my door to find two cops standing there on the porch.

I chalked it up to the kids being especially loud that night. "Everybody quiet down," I instructed them. "You want somebody to call the police again?" And I moved on.

But only a couple weeks went by before I saw a police car roll slowly by my house and shine its spotlight onto my porch. After another couple weeks, we got another knock on the front door.

*Something's going on here*, I thought. I started looking around my street, eyeing my neighbors suspiciously. Back when the kids first showed up at my house and we were all outside together, I'd shout hello to my neighbors as they walked to their cars or watered their flowers. "Yeah, I'm trying to help these kids," I'd tell them in between comments about the weather or how our families were doing.

"That's real nice!" they'd say, smiling at me.

But maybe some of that goodwill had worn off. After all, I had as many as seventy-five kids running in and out of my house at all hours of the night, making trips to the gas station at three in the morning and banging on my door without giving a thought to how late it was.

*Are my neighbors calling the police on me?* I wondered.

Then one night, two detectives burst through my front door. I knew what a detective looked like when I saw one. I'd seen plenty walk through my neighborhood over the years. But I'd never seen these two.

The detectives didn't say a word as they strode into the house. The kids scrambled like cockroaches when the kitchen light gets switched on. Nobody made a sound, but I could see panic in their eyes as they ran from the living room, ducking into bathrooms, closets, out the back door, anywhere they thought they could get away from the detectives.

"Just be still!" I shouted. These kids hadn't done a thing wrong, but I was terrified that all this scrambling would make the detectives suspicious. I'd heard of too many people who had been shot for making sudden movements in a police officer's presence. I didn't want anybody to get arrested or worse. "Don't move. It's alright."

I tried to keep an eye on the detectives and the kids all at once. I watched the detectives walk to the back of the house, turn on their heels, and walk to the front again. *What are these people doing here? Why aren't they talking to me?*

"What's going on?" I demanded, following the detectives to the door. They didn't even acknowledge me as they walked onto the porch and slammed the door behind them.

My house erupted into a roar as soon as the detectives were gone. Every noise the kids had held inside, every fear that gripped them, everything came pouring out as they ran to me from their hiding places. They peppered me with questions so quickly I couldn't respond.

"Miss Diane, what was going on?" somebody yelled.

"Who was they looking for? I'm telling you, Miss Diane, they was looking for somebody."

"I know that one detective, Miss Diane. He bad!"

I forced myself to let go of my own fears, my own panic. The kids didn't need me to freak out. They needed me to be a calming presence. So I put my hands on their shoulders.

"They didn't do anything," I said in the most soothing voice I could muster. "They left. Nobody got hurt. We okay."

I sat with the kids for hours, listening to their fears and their feelings. The whole time, one thought was in the back of my mind. *The police commander is gonna hear about this.*

I climbed into my 1996 Cadillac Sedan DeVille the next morning and drove over to 111th Street to the police district office. "Sending detectives to my house, scaring these kids to death," I muttered under my breath as I steered my car down Michigan Avenue and waited at the stoplight. Those kids told me they honestly thought they might get shot when the detectives walked through my house. Whatever was going on, Commander Ball would fix it. I'd met him several times at Neighborhood Recovery Initiative events, and I'd even had my picture taken with him. He was a great guy. I didn't have an appointment, but I knew he'd take the time to speak with me anyway.

I marched into the commander's office, startling him out of his chair. I wasn't sure if he was surprised to see me or if he had just never seen me look that upset. I was too heated to sit down. I launched into my tirade, telling him all about how those detectives walked in and out of my house without so much as a hello. Commander Ball promised he'd look into it, but I could tell from the creases in his forehead that something else was going on.

The commander sighed. "Miss Latiker, your neighbors are calling the police on you," he said.

"Neighbors? Like, more than one? Well, what are they calling the police for?"

"You've got teenagers hanging around your house. They're probably scared." He said it as kindly as he could, but the words still hurt. All these people, these neighbors who acted like they thought it was so great that I was helping these kids, were actually scared of them.

"Try to keep the kids inside," Commander Ball said. "Then I don't think you'll see any more detectives."

I shook my head slowly. "They come and go," I told him. "I can't lock them in my house. And I'm not going to stop them from coming in."

Commander Ball raised his eyebrows. "Well, they'll probably keep calling then."

I walked out of that office feeling completely alone. Even a good man like Commander Ball couldn't help me. He couldn't make me any promises. And I couldn't exactly ask my neighbors to stop calling. The last thing I wanted was for them to know I'd visited the district and found out they'd called.

It took every ounce of willpower I had to smile and wave over the chain-link fence like nothing had happened whenever I saw my neighbors outside. I couldn't hide from them. Anytime I was outside with the kids, I'd see neighbors leaving for work or coming home, heading to the grocery store or going for a drive. I wanted to shout, "You hate children! You should be over here helping me, not calling the police!" But I held my tongue. What good would it do to start a war with my neighbors? And truth be told, I might have done the same thing if I were in their shoes.

The police kept stopping by. They kept shining their spotlight at my house. I tried my best to shut down each incident with my most respectful tone. And when I saw my neighbors, I kept smiling and waving just like nothing had happened.

Inside my house, tensions were just as high as they were outside. James still didn't like what I was doing. He never made that a secret. I kept hoping he would see what it meant to the kids, that he would learn to love them too.

He tolerated the kids tearing up our living room furniture, eating his food, and taking over every room but our bedroom. There was just one thing off limits—his big-screen TV.

James had wanted a big screen for his football games and *Sanford and Son* reruns for as long as I'd known him. When I started doing hair, we decided to make it happen. We'd put away a hundred dollars here, fifty dollars there, until we'd finally saved up enough. James was so proud when we hauled it home from the store. This was long before the days of flat-panel big screens that one person can lift on their own. This thing practically needed a moving crew to carry it up our front steps and into the dining room. It took up half the room, but James didn't care. He set up his La-Z-Boy recliner in front of it and kicked back like he was king of the castle.

But after I started KOB, I started eyeing that TV like a cash cow. Now that the kids were back in school, they needed computers and printers to write papers, research topics, and get help with homework. I figured I needed at least ten computers and a few printers. And I needed some money to get them.

*Oh, Lord, I gotta ask James if I can sell the TV*, I thought. I waited until I fixed him a nice breakfast on Saturday, hoping to butter him up. But James cut me off as soon as I asked the question.

"Uh-uh," he said shortly. "Nope."

I don't give up that easily. So a few days later, I tried again. And again. And again. Over and over for about two weeks. James's answer never changed.

"Don't you touch that TV," he said. But James knew me. He knew that when I wanted to do something, I'd do it and suffer the consequences.

So one day, after James left for work, I picked up the phone and dialed the number of a TV resale store. The man who answered the phone said he couldn't tell me how much he'd give me for the TV without looking at it, but he'd stop by in an hour. I looked at the clock and felt my forehead start to sweat. "Well, you gotta hurry up," I told him.

True to his word, the man showed up and gave James's TV the once-over.

"I'll give you $600 for it," he said.

"Sold," I said. I signed some papers, he gave me the money, and a crew hauled the TV away. Now I was left to wait on pins and needles until James got home. I paced across the empty space where the TV once stood. *James is gonna kill me*, I thought.

That evening, James opened the door and immediately noticed it was gone. I expected him to yell. Instead, he gave me a look I've only seen maybe three times in our marriage. We carried on this wordless conversation, James's face saying, "You better not have sold that TV," and mine saying, "I sold the TV—I'm so sorry!" That big empty space between us where the TV once stood felt like the Grand Canyon.

When James opened his mouth to speak, it wasn't quiet. James is loud to begin with, but in twenty years I'd never heard him yell like this.

"Why the *so-and-so* did you do that?" he shouted. He never uses profanity unless he's truly angry. "I asked you not to do this. You did it anyway. I should divorce you for this." Sweat beaded on his forehead. "I'm thinking about it, anyway, because I can't take this anymore."

All I could do was stand there like a child, taking my whooping. Nothing I said would matter until he calmed down. All I could say was, "I'm sorry," over and over.

I tried popping my head in the bedroom later that night, when I thought he'd cooled off.

"You still love me?" I asked. He just stared at me blankly.

It wasn't until the next night that he eased up. He told me he was still mad. I said I was sorry, that it wouldn't happen again. We fell back into our routine. I got some computers, and the kids had a place to do homework. I wondered if I'd hurt my case for KOB with James for good. I had thought for sure he'd stop tolerating KOB and start supporting it. Now that I'd sold his TV, that might never happen.

Now, I knew there were some rumblings among my children. A few of them had made it known over those first couple of months of KOB that they weren't exactly thrilled. One of my older daughters let me know in no uncertain terms that she thought the KOB kids were a bunch of thugs and gangbangers who had no business in my house. Even Aisha was nursing a grudge. I didn't find out she didn't like sharing me with the other kids until she told a reporter who was doing a story on KOB.

After a little while, the waves settled. Aisha and I found our groove. I stopped seeing that little jealous frown on her face. And none of my other kids had complained, at least not in a while.

And then, five of them staged a coup. It was the winter after I'd started KOB, and one of my daughters was visiting from out of state. I didn't have a thought in my mind beyond being happy to see her and my grandchildren. When my other kids gathered at my house one night, I figured they just wanted to visit their sister. I didn't think anything of it.

My whole house was filled to bursting with young people doing homework, rapping, singing, and dancing. It was the best of both of my worlds. I had my own kids and my KOB kids all under one roof. Then one of my daughters walked into the living room, her arms crossed.

"Ma, could you ask the kids to step outside for a minute?" she asked.

I looked at her like she was crazy. It was winter in Chicago, and half these kids showed up with nothing but a hoodie. "I'm not doing that," I told her.

Her eyes narrowed. "Fine. Can you come to your bedroom then?"

I had a sinking feeling as I sat on the bed. Five of my older children were crowded around me as one of them shut the door.

"Mom, we been talking," one of them said when everybody quieted down.

That's what they always say when they've been gabbing about something behind my back. "Oh yeah?" I asked calmly, pretending I didn't know what was coming. "What's going on?"

"Ma, I ain't got nothing to do with this!" my second oldest daughter said, waving her arms.

Another daughter took a deep breath. "We feel that what you're doing is dangerous. You need to take another look at what you're doing and really think about whether this is a good idea."

I willed my eyes not to roll back in my head like a pouty teenager's.

"You know those kids are in gangs," she continued. "They might hurt you."

"I keep telling Mama that!" another daughter said. "They shouldn't be in her house. It's okay for her to help them, but they shouldn't be in her house. It ain't good for her, and it ain't good for Aisha."

Two of my boys jumped in. Once they get to going, there's no shutting them up. I kept as composed as I could, nodding here and there, but inside I was screaming, *This is my life!* My boys and girls had all moved out, gotten married, had kids, made lives for themselves. I felt like they wanted me to sit around in my house, waiting on James and Aisha hand and foot and twiddling my thumbs until they decided to visit me. They didn't want me to be anything more than their middle-aged mom. I was changing, and they didn't like it—even though it meant I was happy. *You're gone*, I thought. *This is my life. I'm entitled to live my own life*.

But I didn't say any of that. I just listened until they quieted down and looked at me, waiting for me to speak. Finally, I cleared my throat.

"You guys got some good points," I said slowly. "But I started this. I gotta see where it goes."

"But Mama—"

"I believe God gave this to me," I said as I held up my hand to shush them. "If I believe He gave it to me, I believe He will protect me."

The room was suddenly quiet. My oldest finally shook her head. "Mama ain't listening."

She was right. I wasn't. I believed they were dead wrong.

Sometimes I wondered why I kept going when nobody liked what I was doing. Nobody but my mom. I was overworked, exhausted, stressed about what my kids and husband thought about me. But the kids who walked through my front door didn't see any of that. They didn't notice the bags under my eyes or my rumpled hair. All they cared about was that I was there for them when they needed me. And somebody always needed me.

"Miss Diane, I need a ride to school."

"Miss Diane, I'm cold, and I don't got a coat. Can you help me get one?"

"Miss Diane, could I just sit in here for a while?"

I always said yes. Helping them gave me this high I couldn't explain, a high that got me through the exhaustion and stress. My family may not need me as much anymore, but these kids did. I was a safe place for my community, a place where any kid could come, no matter where they came from or what struggles they carried. It didn't matter if nobody else understood, if nobody supported me, if nobody wanted to help me. I was living out God's will. I couldn't stop now.

CHAPTER FIVE

# Midlife Career Change

I can't quite pinpoint the moment I decided I couldn't keep working full time and running Kids Off the Block in my spare time. For one long, exhausting year, I tried to juggle both. I tried to give my clients my full attention, even though I would rather have been in my living room listening to the boys show off their latest rap or in my van driving the girls to dance at a basketball halftime show. I stayed up most of the night listening to young people pour out their hearts and fussing at them to stop running around with the gang that was trying to recruit them.

KOB wasn't just a hobby. It never had been. I was serious about it from the moment I first heard the original ten kids tell me their problems on my living room floor. But I also hadn't expected it to require my attention twenty-four hours a day. When I first asked those kids to come inside my house, I never imagined I'd have teenagers sleeping on my living room floor, calling me in the middle of the night, and meeting me outside the salon every day. KOB went from ten kids to seventy-five in a matter of months. I was basically working two jobs—but one of them took up three-quarters of my day.

Balancing KOB and doing hair, not to mention attempting to be a wife and mother, was killing me. When I was with the kids, I felt this overwhelming sense of euphoria. I felt giddy, like I was a teenager too. But behind the salon chair, my back ached, my feet throbbed, my whole body cried out for rest.

I was wearing myself out to keep working at my mom's salon, and for what? I didn't like doing hair. Truth was, I wasn't even good at it. My clients kept coming back because they liked talking to me, not because I was particularly skilled. The money was good, but I was tired of working a job I didn't care about just for the paycheck.

KOB was my passion. I knew without a doubt that God had called me to help these kids. I felt in my bones that it was time for me to put down my scissors and devote all my time to KOB. I didn't know how we'd get by without my paycheck, but I was willing to take the risk. KOB was worth it. *I'll figure all that out later*, I told myself. *I know the Lord will take care of it.*

Telling my mom I was done styling hair was the easiest conversation I'd ever had. She practically exploded with pride and hugged me, telling me I was doing exactly what God wanted me to do. Telling James was a different story. He'd finally forgiven me for selling the TV and even stopped complaining about his house being the home of KOB. Now here I was again, making huge decisions without discussing them with him. I know I should have talked to him first. But at the time, I felt this intense urgency to make KOB my full-time job. I knew I'd never convince him to say yes if I ran it by him first. So I didn't.

I meant to break it to him gently that night after most of the kids had left for the day and the others were asleep. I figured I'd rub his shoulders, get him all relaxed, and then tell him the news. But like usual, I was giddy and hyped up after being with the kids all evening. I was babbling on about how Isiah was making friends and coming out of his shell when it just slipped out.

"That's why I can't keep doing hair and doing KOB," I said. "These kids need all of my attention."

James frowned at me suspiciously, his eyebrows raised. "Yes, you can."

"No, I can't," I said slowly. "And I'm not."

"What do you mean you're not?"

"I mean, I quit today. I told my mama I can't do it anymore."

There was that look again—the same look I'd seen the day I sold the TV. Out came the curse words and the word *divorce*.

I was sick of feeling alone, like I was battling against my own husband, when all I was doing was following God's call on my life. So this time, I fought back.

"You need to shut up, talking to me like that," I snapped. "Why can't you just support me?"

James is always loud, but for a moment I was afraid he'd wake the whole neighborhood. "What you mean, I don't support you?" he shouted. "I drive these kids to school. I let them take over my house. And don't you forget my TV paid for their computers. I put up with all of it. And now you just go and quit a good job without even talking to me."

"I'm just following my heart."

"Well, that ain't gonna feed us," he shot back.

"Don't you believe in God?" I searched his face, looking for any hope and understanding at all. I didn't find it. "God's gonna take care of us."

"Yeah, but God didn't tell you to be a fool."

*Oh boy*, I thought. *What did he have to say that for?*

I must confess, I said a few curse words in response. I had to ask the Lord for forgiveness later. The argument exploded into an all-out blowup, with both of us saying nasty things we'd regret later. I don't like to go to bed angry, but I sure did that night.

For days, James and I didn't speak beyond a "What's for dinner?" or "What time you getting home today?" I tried fixing chicken just the way he liked it for dinner and letting him watch his *Sanford and Son* reruns without complaining. He wasn't letting me off the hook that easily.

James couldn't avoid KOB. The kids were there as soon as he walked in the front door from work and sometimes even when he woke up in the morning. And when I needed him to drive someone home or pick up a kid from school, he never said no.

If the kids knew he didn't want them there, they never let on.

"Hey, Mr. J!" they'd yell.

After the first few months, instead of walking straight to the bedroom, he'd hang around the living room and talk with the boys. They'd lay out laughing, listening to James's Mississippi drawl as he said, "What's up, maaaaan?" dragging out the *A* sound.

Eventually, it was the kids that wore him down. I knew it would be. The more they yelled his name and laughed at his jokes, the more James hung around. These city kids thought my country man said the most outrageous stuff, like, "Give me five on the black-hand side!"

Before long, James was singing Luther Vandross along with the boys and crooning the old songs by The Whispers he'd wooed me with years before. Once, he even danced just like

Rick James as he sang "Super Freak" right there in our living room. He had those kids rolling like he was a professional comedian. I felt hopeful. James was warming up to the kids. Was our yearlong standoff finally coming to an end?

One night, I walked in the front door to the scent of garlic and tomatoes. There was James, in the kitchen with his sleeves rolled up, cooking up a big batch of spaghetti and meatballs.

"Food's ready," he said matter-of-factly. I could tell he was proud of himself. But for once, I had no intention of taking him down a peg. I was too busy trying not to burst into tears of joy. James was on his feet all day long fixing cars at the body shop. He was tired too. Instead of complaining that I was out running around with the kids and not making him dinner, he took over without saying a word. He stood behind the stove, dishing up plates of pasta and hollering at the kids to wash their hands, and I finally felt like he was standing behind me and KOB. Maybe we wouldn't fight over this forever. Maybe I wouldn't be on my own anymore. Maybe, just maybe, we'd be partners in this together.

"Oooh, Mr. James, that's good!" Jamal called out from the table.

"You mean you stopped talkin' long enough to eat?" James shouted back. Even Jamal couldn't help but laugh at that one.

From then on, it wasn't unusual for the kids and I to come home to steaming pots of chicken and gravy or platters of Dagwood sandwiches. We'd be outside and hear the sizzle and crackle of hot oil moments before the scent of fried chicken drifted through the window. It was all I could do to keep them from snatching chicken from the pan.

When he wasn't in the kitchen, James was throwing loads of laundry in the washing machine and folding pants and shirts for kids who didn't have clean clothes. He'd buy shoes on his way home for a boy who had worn through the soles of his sneakers.

Then Aisha let it slip that James fixed cars and knew how to build a house from the ground up. Those kids wouldn't leave him alone after that. Our phone just about rang off the hook.

"Mr. James, can you fix my mama's car?"

"Mr. James, can you come fix our cabinets?"

"Mr. James, we got water coming in our basement!"

James grumbled as he tied on his work boots and loaded his toolbox into the car, but I could tell his chest was a little puffed out. I wasn't the only person these kids needed. They needed him too.

He never asked for payment, but he didn't do the work for free. Anybody who asked for help had to work right next to him and learn to do it themselves. James always came home fussing about how Richard couldn't tell an engine from a transmission or how Corey didn't know how to hold a hammer.

"Diane, do you know they didn't even know what a thermostat was?" he yelled. At least it sounded like he was yelling, even if he didn't mean to. "They didn't even know what a stairwell was called!"

"Well, how are they supposed to know that if nobody ever told them?" I said, trying not to laugh.

James grumbled and nodded. "Well, I guess you got a point."

The kids saw through his gruff exterior. They'd fuss and argue when James went after them for breaking the front light in our van or bending a nail when they tried to hammer. But a moment later, they'd ask him to say one of his Mississippi sayings, and they'd all be rolling on the floor laughing. He was in the center of the action, joking with the boys or explaining how to change a tire. *He gets it*, I thought. *He knows why we have to help these kids. He loves them just as much as I do.*

For months, I'd prayed that God would soften my husband's heart, that we wouldn't be adversaries anymore, that he would be just as committed to KOB as I was. I shouldn't have been surprised that God answered my prayer. It wasn't His first answer, and it most definitely wouldn't be His last.

When I was a young woman, I would rather have died than let anyone know I couldn't handle something on my own. Once, when I was married to my first husband, my children and I lived on nothing but rice for a week. We didn't have any money in the bank to shop at the grocery store, and even though my mom would have been more than willing to help, I refused to ask her or anybody else for a dime. *That's not how my mama raised me*, I thought. *I ain't asking nobody for nothing.*

Fast forward to 2004, and my life was a different story. Now that we were living only on James's salary, all pride was out the window. James and I could get by. I knew we'd figure it out. But I wanted to do more for these kids. I wanted them to have matching T-shirts when we cheered at rallies and visited community groups. I wanted a few more basketball goals now that the one we had was already worn out. I wanted more computers so kids wouldn't have to wait as long for a turn to do their homework. I wanted my kitchen stocked with lunch meat, bread, and chips so I could always feed anybody who was hungry. And when I closed my eyes at night, I dreamed of the thing I wanted most—a building to hold KOB. My house was bursting at the seams with the dozens of young people who came through every day. James and I had no privacy, and everything we had, from the furniture to the floors, was worn out from overuse.

*Somebody's gotta help me*, I thought. *Somebody has to see that what we're doing is important. Somebody will want to get involved.*

My first stop was my alderman's office. Everybody said the man who ran our ward for the Chicago City Council had money he could distribute in the community however he saw fit. So I sat in his office waiting for him. Day after day, I kept showing up. I told him about kids who didn't have shoes, kids whose families' lights were turned off, kids who needed a good, hot meal.

After a while, the man got sick of me. He couldn't turn me away. After all, I was his constituent. But he'd make me wait a good, long while, hoping I'd give up and leave. This man did not know that Diane Latiker is stubborn as a mule. I could see him peek through a crack in his office door, take one look at me, and close the door.

"He'll be out in a few minutes," his secretary would say with a smile.

"Okay," I'd say. Minutes would tick by. He wouldn't budge from his office.

"Could you please ask him about what time he'll be out?" I'd finally ask.

She'd disappear behind his door only to reemerge with the same line. "He'll be out in a few minutes."

But once I was finally seated in his office, it was never the magic solution I'd hoped for. He'd listen to my long list of problems, nodding without ever offering a solution. One day, I'd finally had it.

"You're just not gonna help, are you?" I said, my arms crossed.

The man held my gaze. "Yeah, and that's why you're mad, because I won't do what you want me to do and say what you want me to say."

"Oh really?" I locked my eyes on his, daring him to keep talking.

"Do you know somebody got shot right by my office just the other day?" He spun in his chair and frowned at me. "You're out there helping people just like that. You got nothing but gangbangers and thugs in your program. The best thing I can do for them is lock them up."

I couldn't move. This man was supposed to represent my neighborhood. Yet now he was telling me the kids I'd come to love were dangerous, disposable, not worth saving. Nothing I could say would make a lick of difference to him. I gathered my purse and walked out of the office.

Meanwhile, I came up with what I believed was a brilliant plan to help KOB. I would write a letter to Oprah. Her talk show ruled daytime television, her book club determined which novel would be the next bestseller, and anything on her "Oprah's Favorite Things" list suddenly became impossible to find in stores. As far as I was concerned, Oprah was the queen. If Oprah knew what I was trying to do, she would help me.

My heart raced with excitement as I put pen to paper and scrawled out my dreams for KOB and how I wanted to help get the young people of Roseland off the street and into college and the workforce. I told her how desperately I needed somebody of her stature to help me guide these kids. I asked for a building, a van, computers, everything short of the moon. The assistant who read my letter probably thought, "This lady is crazy."

Two weeks went by without a response. I wasn't deterred. I sat down and wrote another letter. And when that didn't get a response, I wrote another. I felt like a kid writing to Santa Claus, refusing to believe the mounting evidence that he wasn't real. The chances of my letter ever making it past the workers sifting through Oprah's piles of mail and onto Oprah's desk were extremely slim.

*I gotta get real*, I finally told myself. *Maybe Oprah isn't the answer. Maybe there are other resources out there.*

I started with the churches. I walked up the block to St. John Missionary Baptist Church and talked to the pastor about what we were trying to do for the kids in our neighborhood. Next thing I knew, he took a special offering for us one Sunday. Metropolitan Baptist Services members donated notepads and journals.

Then I met a man named Joseph Strickland, who turned out to be *the* man. He knew everybody in the nonprofit world and didn't waste any time introducing me to people, telling organizations what I needed, and stopping at my house to visit with the kids. That man was incredible. I also met a young man named Syron Smith, who was also working to stop violence throughout Chicago and was just getting started forming his organization, National Block Club University. Syron connected me to the people funding his group and helped me get funds from them too.

I was blown away. I knew how hard it was to find funding. These people could have kept their funders a secret and left me to fend for myself. Instead, they took me under their wing. Because of them, I started partnering with groups like Magic and CeaseFire that also worked with Chicago's young people. I had money to buy food, shoes, pants, coats, whatever the kids needed. I could tell that the group leaders thought I was unorganized, and they weren't wrong. I may have been a year into this, but I was still smack in the middle of figuring things out. So when I met group leaders who seemed like they had it going on, I latched on to them. I watched how they ran their programs, tracked their outcomes, and reached out to the community.

But everywhere I went, I heard the same criticism. "These kids are dangerous," I was told by everybody from pastors to nonprofit founders. It turned out, most people wanted to work with the "good kids," the ones staying in school and out of gangs, the ones who were less risky, easier to love. Some organizations—even churches—refused to work with me because of who I helped.

I thought of DaJuan selling drugs to put food on the table for his family, Isiah joining a gang to walk to school without constantly looking over his shoulder. *Aren't these exactly the kinds of kids we should be helping?* I thought. *Why are people treating them like they're throwaway kids?*

Arguing was a waste of my time. So I kept my mouth shut. I knew there was only one way to change their minds. *I'm gonna prove them wrong*, I told myself. *I'm gonna show up for these kids. I'm gonna show them there's another way to live beyond the streets, beyond the gangs, beyond the violence. I'll show everybody.*

# Around the Clock

"Tick, tick, tick."

The clock mounted on the wall was the only noise in the police department save for the buzzing fluorescent lights. I checked the time and sighed, settling back into my plastic chair. Two thirty in the morning. Way too late, even by my night-owl standards.

Earlier, at 1:00 a.m. while some of the kids and I were working on a new song, the phone at my house started ringing. My stomach dropped. When the phone rings after ten o'clock, it's never good news.

DaJuan's voice was on the other end. "Miss Diane, I'm locked up." He sounded calm, like it wasn't the first time he'd made a call like this.

"What? What happened?"

"I was in the car with some guys, and they just got me too. I didn't do nothing."

*Yeah, sure*, I thought, remembering all the nights I'd seen him standing on the neighborhood street corner. "Where are you?"

I heard DaJuan cover the mouthpiece as he asked somebody in the background. "I'm over here in Oak Lawn."

*Oh, Lord. What is he thinking getting into trouble in Oak Lawn?* Everybody knew you don't ride through Oak Lawn with so much as an expired plate if your skin is brown. The Chicago suburb may have been only twenty-five minutes from Roseland, but anybody from our neighborhood stuck out like a sore thumb on the tree-lined streets of the upscale, mostly white community. If that's where DaJuan was, I couldn't just leave him there. I'd heard about what happens to kids like DaJuan in jail. This was a crisis, and I had to get there as fast as possible.

I had already changed into my jogging pants and hoodie that night. I wasn't about to get dressed up just to sit in some police station, so I slipped on my gym shoes, tied a bandana around my head, and headed out the door, James grumbling behind me. He insisted on driving me, and even though I put up a fight, secretly I was thankful. I wasn't too keen on driving in Oak Lawn this late at night alone.

"Why didn't he call his mama?" James fussed. "What's he doing calling you? You got your own problems to deal with."

I shook my head. "I don't know. But he in trouble and we got to go."

The man in the metal window sneered at me when I walked through the police department door. I knew he was sizing me up in my do-rag and hoodie, dressed like a teenage boy. I probably looked like a thug to him. *You're one of them*, I imagined him thinking.

"I'm looking for DaJuan Jacobson, sir," I said as politely as I could. I folded my hands, waiting as he typed rapidly into the computer in front of him.

"Who are you?" the man snapped at me.

"I'm his mentor." I knew better than to snap back. You don't get anywhere treating the police with disrespect.

The man shook his head. "You can't see him."

"I can't see him?" I frowned. I thought anybody could bail someone out of jail. Or at least, that's how it worked on the TV shows I watched at home with James.

"No." The man almost seemed delighted to turn me away. "There's nothing you can do because you're not related."

Slowly, I turned around and headed to the plastic chairs lining the walls. Pulling out my old-school cell phone, I dialed DaJuan's home number and braced myself for an uncomfortable conversation. His mama and I had a tense relationship. When DaJuan started coming to KOB, I thought she was just worn out from being a single mom. It wasn't until later that I learned DaJuan came home telling her all about the things I said he should and shouldn't do. She didn't like that so much, and she didn't like me either.

After a couple tries, I finally got ahold of her. I told her DaJuan was locked up in Oak Lawn. I figured she'd yell or maybe even cry. Instead, she spoke in the same calm way that DaJuan had.

"Well, how do you know?" she asked flatly.

"He called me."

Wrong thing to say. "Well, I don't know why he didn't call here," she sputtered.

"I don't know, but I'm down here." It took every ounce of willpower not to say, "Lady, it's two in the morning. Really?"

If DaJuan's mom planned on coming to the police department, she didn't say so. I couldn't take off without knowing if DaJuan was getting out or how he was getting home. There was nothing I could do but get as comfortable as I could in my chair and wait. The ticking clock seemed so loud I thought I might scream. I imagined James looking at his watch in the car, muttering to himself that this boy better have something to say for himself when he gets out.

I felt like I'd sat in that police department for an eternity, but it was probably two hours after I arrived that an officer popped his head in the window. I was startled out of my seat.

"He'll be coming out in just a minute," he said.

DaJuan sauntered into the room moments later.

I stood up. "Why did they let you out of there?"

DaJuan shrugged. "They just told me I could go."

I studied him, looking for some sign of remorse or fear. I waited for him to say he was sorry. But he just looked at me as if to say, "What?" Getting locked up didn't faze him like it might have the first time.

I wanted to ask him what in the world he was thinking riding around Oak Lawn with mollies and weed in his pocket. I wanted to demand an explanation and tell him he had some nerve dragging me out in the middle of the night. But I stopped. I thought about how the officer at the window had snapped at me, a person off the street who was just trying to bail someone out. If that's how they treated me, what had they done to DaJuan?

So instead, I shot him my fiercest look. The words "Don't say nothing to me" were stamped all over my face. Between James's fussing and the police officer's attitude, I'd had enough for the night. DaJuan shut right up as he trudged behind me through the parking lot to my DeVille.

Nobody said a word the entire thirty-minute ride home. I still wasn't ready to speak as we climbed out and opened the front door to my house. Aisha and the kids were still up even though it was practically morning.

"Don't say nothing to Miss Diane," DaJuan announced as he walked in. "She mad."

"I'm mad too!" James hollered. "Calling people this time of night. This boy here got some nerve."

I dissolved into laughter. Nobody but this man could make me crack up when I'm fuming.

The truth was, DaJuan wasn't the only kid calling us or knocking on our door in the middle of the night. I told everybody KOB was my full-time job, but that didn't quite describe it. There were no days off, no closing hours. I was working around the clock, every day. Somebody was getting put out of their house late at night for cussing out their parents, or a kid was about to get jumped by a rival gang, or two boys were about to swing fists.

During the day, the house was always open. I served kids up to age twenty-five, so even when school was in session, somebody was always at my house. There was no structure, no hours of service. I just tried to find something to do for whoever was there. If they weren't practicing their raps, songs, and dances, they were huddled in mentoring sessions or out on the lot playing basketball. Sometimes I'd take them outside armed with brooms, rakes, and trash bags, and we'd walk up and down the block cleaning. I was in the gas station almost every day, flanked by a whole crew of kids, coaxing the cashier to donate some juices or chips.

There was no line between KOB and my personal life. KOB was my life. Whether I was running an errand or visiting another group, I always had at least one kid with me. There was always something to do. There was always a call. Maybe someone needed to talk, or somebody got shot and we had to visit him at the hospital, or somebody didn't have shoes and I had to take him shopping. If I wasn't busy meeting a need, I was hitting up my mom, my auntie, my friends, people I'd met at meetings, anyone I could think of who could pitch in a dollar here or there. Somebody always needed a coat or a T-shirt.

I was running on pure adrenaline. I may have been one year into this, but I was still caught up in the euphoria of helping these kids. I still felt a rush every time they filed into my living room or pulled me aside to talk about a problem. I was needed. I had a purpose. I was living out my dream.

When I look back on those days, I can't remember a single time I left the house without a kid in tow. I was like the little old woman who lived in a shoe, I had so many kids I didn't know what to do. That's how I must have looked anyway. Kids who were hanging around my house all piled into the van anytime I left the house, whether I was going to the store or stopping by a block party or community event. We'd roll the windows down and coast down the highway as we blared rap music as loud as we could. I knew just as many rap songs as they did, and I did the dozens right along with them. They knew wherever we went, I'd make sure we had a ball.

But sometimes when we got back, I'd find Aisha standing in the living room, her arms crossed like she'd been waiting for me.

"Can you take me over to the mall to get a new shirt?" she'd ask. When I said no, she stuck her lower lip out just like she did when she was two. She was taller than me by now, but she sure wasn't grown.

"Well, you took Jamal and them shopping. I don't know why you can't take me."

Every day it was a battle with her. I knew she'd moved past wishing I'd never started KOB, but sharing her mama didn't get easier. Seeing me walking around with Jamal, DaJuan, and Richard at my heels stirred some kind of jealousy in her.

"I know these boys, Ma," she told me over and over again. "They do bad things, and you just cater to them."

I never pretended to be their friend. I may have acted like a big kid sometimes, but I treated those kids the same as I did Aisha and my other kids when they were young. I never hesitated to grab my pen and prick these hardened boys for cursing in my house. When their hair got raggedy, I told them they had two choices—they could let me run a lawnmower through their mane, or we could go to the barber shop. And I'd threaten to tie a string around their waist if they let their pants sag. The sight of these boys thinking they were so big and tough as they hitched their pants up every two seconds on the basketball court made me laugh so hard I was crying.

Many of these kids had good moms at home, and some of them even had dads involved in their lives too. I wasn't telling them any different than what some of them were already hearing at home. But there was something about hearing it from somebody else. For some of them, it was the first time they'd had someone in their corner who wasn't their parent. That's why the gangs thrive in our community. These gang leaders give kids this false sense of security, that somebody's watching over them and will take care of them. I realized if I could fill that role, then maybe, just maybe, I could keep some of these kids out of the gangs. Maybe they'd live past their twenties. Maybe they would learn they couldn't solve their problems with a gun.

The kids kept coming. Whether we were in the house or playing basketball on the lot, somebody new would show up. One day, we were out on the lot when I saw a skinny light-skinned boy wearing a Chicago Bulls jersey swaggering toward us. I guessed he was around fifteen years old, but something about his body language made him seem like a grown man. He was confident, but he didn't look friendly. I couldn't tell if he was squinting in the sun or frowning at us.

The other boys froze as he strode onto the court. Everybody gave him a look of recognition like they knew him, but there were no high-fives or fist bumps like when one of their buddies came out to play. Without saying a word, somebody passed him the ball.

"That's TO, Miss Diane," Jessie whispered in my ear on the sidelines. I could hear the fear in her voice. "He's from over there on Yale Street. He's one of those BG boys."

I leaned forward in my folding chair and nodded, watching the other boys move out of TO's way as he dribbled to the hoop. Normally these boys play like they're in the last game of the NBA finals and don't let anybody get to the basket without practically tackling them. TO was clearly a good ball player, but I could tell everybody was going out of their way to give him space. *They're scared*, I thought.

"He been in trouble?" I asked Jessie.

She nodded. "He'll fight anybody over nothing. I heard he beat up somebody with a stick because he lost to them shooting dice in the alley."

I realized I'd heard stories whispered about TO before. The kids all talked about how this boy came from a family of drug dealers. Everybody knew his uncle was a big-time dealer with a literal fortress around his house just two blocks away from me and KOB. I didn't find out until later that TO's father had been shot and injured just the week before TO showed up on the basketball court.

All the other boys may have been scared of him, but I never turned anybody away who wanted to play. *TO's the kind of boy who needs KOB*, I thought. So when the ball went out of bounds and the game stopped, I walked onto the court and introduced myself.

"What's your real name?" I asked him after he told me his nickname.

"I'm Aaron Jeffreys," he said. His voice was deep and firm, adding to his grown-up persona.

"You play ball?" I asked.

He gave me a cocky half-nod. "Yeah, I play ball."

I sat down in my folding chair as one of the boys inbounded the ball. TO had a right to be cocky. The boy had serious skills. He controlled the ball like a yo-yo as he zigzagged across the asphalt, crossing up anybody in his path as he dribbled to the hoop for an easy layup. Even if the boys weren't afraid to touch him, they couldn't have stopped him.

But when the next play didn't go his way, TO cursed at the top of his lungs. I stood up and shook my head.

"Hey, hey!" I called. "You can't curse on the court. I'm sorry but that's my rule."

TO muttered a half-hearted apology before the game started up again. Not two minutes went by before he cursed again. Before I could say a word, Rico was next to him.

"Don't curse no more," he said, his eyes wide as he nodded in my direction. "Miss Diane don't like it."

TO laughed. "Don't nobody tell me what to do."

The other boys' eyes widened as they stared at me, wondering what I would do. They all knew the rules. They'd learned by now that the f-word would earn them a prick with my pen.

I stood up again, this time walking closer to TO. He may have been hard, but I had to show him I was harder. If I let him get away with cursing today, he'd only try to get away with more. Not only that, but the other kids might get the idea that they didn't have to listen to me either.

"Do not curse out here," I said firmly.

TO's eyes narrowed. "You don't own this lot."

"No, but if you keep cursing, I ain't gonna let you play out here no more today."

When another curse word flew out of his mouth, I'd had enough. "You gotta go," I said, taking the ball and standing in the middle of the court. "See you later."

For a moment, I wondered if he'd listen to me or what I'd do if he didn't. I was a little surprised when he walked away, cursing with each step he took. I watched him disappear in the horizon and sighed. I never enjoyed telling a kid to leave. But it was the only way I could get them to respect me and my rules.

He must not have been too mad, though, because the very next day, there he was, walking across the lot again. I smiled when I saw him. This time, TO caught my eye and smiled back sheepishly. "Yeah, I'm back," his face seemed to say.

After apologizing for the day before, TO was back on the court, playing his heart out. Only a few minutes went by before I heard him slip a curse word. The other boys whipped their heads toward me, wondering if I would stop the game. I decided to let this one slide. *He's new*, I thought. *He'll learn.*

But when he dropped the f-word, I was on my feet and in his face. "Now, didn't I say you can't curse?" I demanded.

"Well, I just said—"

"I said don't curse out here." When he couldn't make it through the next play without cursing, I threw him out again.

Day after day, week after week, TO and I repeated the same scene over and over. He'd apologize, I'd let him play, he'd curse again, I'd throw him out.

"That slipped, Miss Diane," he'd say.

"Miss Diane, that was only 'cause he hit me in my jaw." Nobody bought that one. Nobody would dare to hit that boy in his jaw. TO was learning. I could see he was starting to respect me. But I had to let him know he couldn't walk all over me. Every day when he left, I'd hold my breath and pray that he'd be back the next day. Sure enough, he'd make the walk of shame back to the court the next time we were out on the lot.

Finally, TO came to the lot one day and stood in front of me, frowning. "Miss Diane, I been thinking about this."

"Is that a good or bad thing?" I asked.

He shrugged. "My family, that's just how they talk. That's what I grew up around. I'm not trying to disrespect you. I just can't help it."

I looked into his brown eyes and put my hand on his shoulder. "I understand. But TO, you can't do that here. It's disrespecting me, and it's disrespecting all the other boys."

"They all curse!" he protested.

I nodded. "Yeah, they do, but not around me."

I didn't even think he listened. But when somebody fouled him that day or he missed a shot, he gritted his teeth and didn't say a word. I crossed my arms and smiled, satisfied. *You're not too tough to listen to a little old short lady*, I thought.

When the sun sank low in the sky and long shadows fell across the lot, I stood up and folded up my chair. "Let's head on in," I hollered.

I watched as TO helped the other boys roll the basketball hoop across the street and chain it to the porch. I figured he was only there to play basketball, yet there he was walking into my house and flopping down on the living room floor. The other kids looked at him warily. Truth was, I was just as surprised as they were.

I felt my heart swell as TO caught my eye from across the room and grinned at me. *Lord, how on earth did You bring this boy here?* I prayed. *I gotta help this boy. Help me get him off the street. There's no telling what he could do if we can just get him on the right path.*

# Save a Teen

"Alright, y'all line up behind me! We getting ready for the next take!"

At least half a dozen boys wearing their KOB T-shirts formed a semicircle behind me on the Curtis Elementary gym floor. A director who'd made videos for local rappers set up lights around us and told the cameraman where to stand. TO smirked as I smoothed my hair and tucked in my white shirt airbrushed with the KOB logo.

"Miss Diane, you really rappin' in this video?" he laughed.

I rolled my eyes. "Boy, you hush before I prick you with my pen," I said. "You know I can rap better than you."

One of the new boys, Donnie, burst out laughing. "Man, you know she right." Even TO's fiercest look couldn't shut him up.

"That ain't rapping," DaJuan said. "That's perpetrating. She oughtta get locked up for rapping like that."

I tried not to laugh. Those kids weren't shy about telling me what they thought when I rapped at the top of my lungs in the van. And they weren't wrong. I was under no illusions about my future as a rap star. But our producer was adamant. If I wanted to get my song "Save a Teen / Do Something" out into the world and encourage young people, I'd have to get a little uncomfortable.

I pulled the lyric sheet I'd printed that morning out of my pocket and looked at the lyrics one last time. With each word, the anger I'd felt two years earlier rushed back. I could still see Levi and Creson on my porch back in 2003 when KOB had only been going for a few months.

It was well past ten o'clock when I heard a knock. My front door was open to let some of the cool night air into the stuffy house, but the screen was locked since it was so late. I must have had at least twenty kids in the living room alone, so I'm not sure how I even noticed the noise.

I opened the door to find Levi flanked by his partner in crime, Creson.

"You boys want to come inside?" I asked.

They shook their heads. "Miss Diane, we need to talk to you," Levi said in a hushed voice.

I'd known Levi since he and his family moved into the house next door a few months earlier. That boy was barely old enough to drive, but from morning until late at night, he did nothing but smoke weed and drink. Word spread around fast that anybody who stopped by could take a hit or grab a drink. Next thing I knew, boys who'd been at KOB every single day were stopping by his house instead.

I'd worked too hard with these kids to lose them now. No way was I going to let them go without a fight. I'd marched over there one day when I saw Levi outside and asked him to stop getting the kids in my program into trouble. Apparently, that was the wrong move. From then on, every time one of Levi's sisters saw me, they were in my face, yelling and cussing and telling me to stay out of their business.

"Just go on over there in your house, old lady!" they'd yell. Now I had this kid luring my boys right back into the kind of life I had worked to save them from, plus a full-fledged family feud on my hands. Every night, I'd pace the floor, wringing my hands and lifting my prayers up to the Lord. I needed to stop this boy from poaching the kids from my program, but I had no idea how to do it.

This feud went on for weeks until one day, I noticed Levi's thirteen-year-old brother, Darrell, out in the yard. When a few of my KOB boys told him they were headed inside to record one of their raps, he sighed.

"Man, I really wanna do some music."

A lightbulb switched on in my head. *Maybe I can win Levi over through his brother*, I thought.

"Well, you oughtta come over here," I called from the yard.

Darrell raised his eyebrows and twisted his mouth doubtfully. "Oh, you got something I can make music with?"

"We got a whole studio!" Now I had his attention. "Come on over here and see it."

Darrell looked around for a moment, I guessed to make sure nobody in his family was looking. Satisfied that he was alone, he shrugged and followed me into the tiny room that used to be my spare bedroom.

His eyes lit up as I opened the door. It wasn't much—just a track recorder, an electric piano, and a computer app with every instrument imaginable. A few pieces of foam hung on the dark blue walls to keep the sound of rowdy kids out of the recordings, and an old microphone and headphones sat on a tiny table. All of it was used and dusty, donated from a guy in Indiana who'd heard of us. None of it was shiny or impressive. But Darrell's mouth hung open in awe, as if this little studio was the most beautiful sight he'd ever seen.

"That's actually pretty cool," he admitted.

"Go on and try it out if you want." I pulled out a chair and motioned for him to sit down.

Minutes later, Darrell was behind the computer, the headphones on, lost in his music and oblivious to the world around him. This boy could create original music from scratch just as naturally as he brushed his teeth and washed his face. I couldn't believe he was only thirteen.

"You got a gift," I told him, my eyes sincere. "You can come back here anytime you want and hang out in my studio."

I didn't need to tell him twice. Darrell was back the very next day, helping the other boys create tracks for their raps and manning the studio like he'd been running it his whole life. Every day, he was there. He couldn't have resisted the music if he'd tried.

I wasn't surprised when Levi showed up on my doorstep a few days later. He cut right to the chase without so much as a hello.

"Where Darrell at?" he asked flatly.

I pointed behind me. "He over there in the studio," I said. I'll admit I was short with him. I'd had too many arguments with Levi to welcome him with open arms and give him a big smile. But I let him come in.

Levi made his way to the back room and went inside. I kept checking the door, waiting for him to come out. I figured he just wanted to make sure his little brother was okay. But minutes ticked by, and there was still no sign of him.

Finally, I stuck my head inside the studio to check on them. There was Levi, sitting next to Darrell, grinning and bobbing his head to the music. Darrell leaned into the computer with his headphones on, focused on the notes and beats. When the music stopped, Levi burst into applause.

"That was great, bro!" he said, patting Darrell on the back. He beamed at him like a little kid, smiling from ear to ear.

"It was okay." Darrell tried to shrug away his brother's compliment.

"Naw, I'm serious. You good at this. You need to keep it up."

From then on, when Darrell showed up at KOB, Levi was with him. There were no more arguments, no more disagreements. He and I had made peace. I still kept my eye on him. The other kids whispered he was a trigger man, someone who would shoot if he had the opportunity. They said he was in a gang back in wherever he was from before he moved to Chicago, which meant he had no protection here on the streets. When he wasn't at KOB, he was into it with one of the gangs—that is if he wasn't drinking or getting high. But when he was in my house, he followed the rules. He played it cool. He even let me cast him in a play as a gang leader named Big O.

Until he showed up on my porch that night with his buddy Creson. They looked around, like they were making sure nobody was listening.

Levi and Creson were quite the pair. Levi was fearless, tough, hotheaded. Creson just wasn't made from the same stock, much as he tried to be. He wanted to be in the mix, to prove that he was just as hard as Levi. But when it came right down to it, he was scared. He needed Levi because if he actually got into a dangerous situation, he didn't have what it took to pull the trigger.

"What are you boys doing out here?" I said to them. "Don't y'all realize how late it is?"

"Miss Diane, we gotta tell you something." Levi's voice was quiet as he looked over my shoulder to see who was close by.

"Well, what is it?"

Creson motioned for me to come outside. Now I was worried. I closed the screen door behind me and stepped closer to the boys.

Levi leaned toward me like he was about to tell me a secret. "We got that meat, Miss Diane."

I stepped back and frowned. "You got what?" I'd been surrounded by teenagers for months, and I'd still never heard anything like that.

"We got the gun, Miss Diane." Creson was practically smiling, like he was proud. "We gonna get 'em."

A thousand questions flew through my head. Who gave these teenagers a gun? What were they thinking? And why in the world would they tell me about it? Did they think I'd give them a high-five and send them on their way? Or, deep down, did they want me to stop them?

"Oh, no you not," I said, confused.

Both boys stumbled all over themselves in protest. "Miss Diane, they shouldn't have did what they did!" Levi sputtered.

"They came at us." Creson waved his hands around, as if somehow he could make me understand his point of view. "They was finna do something. So now we finna show them—"

"You ain't finna do nothing," I shouted over them as my heart pounded. I could feel the blood rising in my cheeks. I'd turned my whole world upside down just to get kids off the street. I wanted them out of gangs, away from the violence that kept our community trapped indoors like we lived in a war zone. Hearing these boys talk about running out and shooting somebody like it was nothing made me feel like I cared more about keeping them alive than they cared about keeping themselves alive.

"Are you trying to go to jail?" I demanded. Their eyes grew wide, and I could tell they wished they'd never knocked on my door. "Are you trying to die? You don't bring that mess here. This is my house. You want to go out and get yourselves killed, go ahead. But get off my porch."

"Oh, Miss Diane!" they protested. By now, a few kids had appeared in the doorway to find out what was going on. I knew I had to get them out of there. The last thing I wanted was another kid to get ideas from these fools.

When they finally left and walked back to Levi's house, I slammed the door behind me. All I felt in that moment was anger. Anger at their complete lack of respect for themselves and others. Anger that the violence that should have scared them had become normal. Anger that shooting somebody seemed like a reasonable way for them to solve a disagreement.

Summer is always bloody in Chicago. When the weather heats up, so do tensions between gangs. Crosses pop up on street corners like perennial flowers. Families stay inside, scared of getting caught in the cross fire. During the summer of 2003, we'd seen so many people shot that our city became the homicide capital of the country.

Nobody was untouched by it. Every kid in KOB had a brother, cousin, uncle, father, friend, friend of a friend, somebody who had been shot—if they hadn't been shot themselves.

Even on my own street, my family and I had hit the floor during drive-by shootings. This was Roseland. This was the world as the kids knew it. It was normal to expect that you'd probably get shot or locked up before your twenty-fifth birthday. It was normal that if somebody said something you didn't like, you'd ride by their house shooting out their windows. It was normal not to bother dreaming of a life beyond selling drugs and riding with your gang. They didn't know life could be any different. Some of these kids had literally never even been to downtown Chicago. They'd never left the four blocks that surrounded them. This was their whole world.

I'd seen the terror on these kids' faces. I was there when Kenneth Easton ran into my house and slammed the door behind him, panic written all over his face. He told me his friend had been killed, and he was terrified that whoever shot his friend was after him too. This wasn't some kid feeling paranoid. At the same time I was consoling him, I was looking out the window, wondering if the guys with guns might follow him to my house.

The people in charge had written off every block and left them to rot. These kids had no hope. No power. No power but a gun, in their minds. That's why Levi and Creson looked proud to tell me they got that meat. Somebody, whatever they did, had made them feel scared, small, powerless. Now nobody would dare mess with them. Now they had something.

I pictured Levi's face and felt the rage rising inside me all over again. I thought about how they'd practically smiled as they told me about their big plans to go throw away their lives and take away somebody else's in the process. And for what? Because they were mad? These boys were off their rockers. Yet they were looking at me like I was crazy because I wanted them to stay alive, stay out of trouble, and make good lives for themselves. I felt alone, like I was the only one who cared about saving these kids.

I marched past the other kids and into my bedroom. My hands shook as I pulled my raggedy spiral notebook out of my nightstand drawer and picked up a pen. All the rage, all the frustration, came pouring out in that moment. I didn't know exactly what I was writing or what I would do with it. I just needed to get these feelings out.

I'd never planned to show anyone what I'd written. But when my music-producer brother-in-law caught me hunched over my notebook, I ended up reading it to him. That winter, we put my poem to music. And two years later, there we were in the gym, making a music video, waiting for the cameraman to roll the tape.

The director yelled, "Action!" I forgot where I was. I forgot how the kids laid out laughing at my attempts at rapping. The only thing in my head was the lyrics. I swayed as the track played behind me.

> Come on, people, let's do something
> Don't you wanna do something?
> Save a teen.

The song told the story of the night Levi and Creson stood on my porch telling me they got that meat. I rapped everything I'd said that night and everything I wished I had said.

> I asked them, do they know what it means for their
> finger to be on the trigger . . .

Giving it a sexy name like, "I got that meat"
Letting everybody know they gon' ride or die
Willing to let their blood run in the streets for a
concrete block that don't belong to them

Every nerve or ounce of self-consciousness disappeared. I looked straight into the camera and yelled that these kids were wasting their lives getting high and riding with their crew.

It's not cool to be successful and do good
You know it's true when the drug dealer is the hero in
your neighborhood

At the end of the song, I wasn't rapping anymore. I was preaching. It was everything I had ever wanted to say to these kids, to their parents, to the world. This was my plea, my passion, my mission.

Man, it makes me mad
Because what we have done is set our children up to
be disgraced
Losing a whole generation
Our young men are leaving this nation
Where's our marching, protest, outrage at the loss of
our teens?
Don't you wanna do something?
Don't you wanna do anything?

When we finished recording, the kids and I laughed and high-fived one another. I smiled at the boys in the semicircle. That day, I didn't know that some of the kids standing behind me couldn't be saved. I didn't know some of them would be gunned down before they were old enough to vote. I didn't know some of them would spend decades of their lives locked up for murder. I was blissfully unaware of what lay ahead. We headed back to my house like it was a normal day of KOB. Because as far as we knew, it was.

CHAPTER EIGHT

# "It's Your Vision"

I tore open the envelope as soon as I saw it sitting in my mailbox. After weeks of waiting, I would finally find out if a grant would help me add new programs to KOB.

Three years into this thing, I thought we had it going on. Dozens of kids were in and out of my house every single day. These young people weren't just talking about riding with their crew or getting high anymore. They were talking about the future. Some of them even mentioned college. I had Jamal, Corey, and Tetey out performing at events in the community. I had kids dancing at basketball games.

All the partnerships I'd tried to build over the years were paying off. A police officer had donated an old van, and every chance we got, I piled those kids into the van and we took off, rolling into CeaseFire cookouts on blocks that had just experienced violence. By now, I'd loaded a couple dozen kids into buses and taken them out to Minnesota, St. Louis, and

Atlanta with National Block Club University. If these kids were going to learn about the world outside of their little four-block radius, they needed to see it for themselves. I even had Public Allies in my house hosting workshops on how to organize and impact our community.

James and I had long since stopped battling about KOB. He was right by my side watching the kids on the basketball court, showing them how to fix cars, and hollering at them when they got out of line. We still didn't have any privacy, and KOB dominated our lives around the clock, but compared to when we'd started, life was good.

I was riding high. I could see the changes in these kids from the way they looked me in the eye, from the way they talked, from their body language. But what I didn't have—and what every grant and partner seemed to want—were concrete outcomes. Including the grant whose letter I held in my hand that day. I ripped open the envelope only to read the familiar words: "We regret to inform you . . ."

I didn't get it. Again. My lack of outcome came back to bite me once more. At this point, I'd heard the same story so many times I didn't even have the energy to be disappointed.

Whether I was filling out a grant application or making small talk at a nonprofit event, it all came down to numbers. They wanted results they could measure. How many kids had dropped out of gangs? How many kids stayed in school? How many shootings did we have in our neighborhood this year compared to the year before?

I didn't know how to explain that what I was doing couldn't be boiled down to statistics. In our neighborhood, it's more complicated than that. It's messy. I could mentor these kids and talk to them about dreaming for the future and staying away from gangs until I was blue in the face. But I couldn't take them out of their home lives, their streets, or the groups of kids surrounding them. Even if they changed their minds, sometimes they were still trapped by their circumstances.

Like Corey. Corey was still a kid of the neighborhood. He was friends with boys in just about every gang in Roseland. His cousin, Malcom, and his best friend, Sean, were in rival gangs, and Corey was in the middle of all of them. Sometimes, when one of the gangs had an issue with another, they'd call Corey and expect him to ride with them—*ride* almost always meant a drive-by. Corey never said no. Even though he wasn't a member, part of Corey secretly wished he were a gangster. But by now, his desire to become a singer was even stronger.

From the first time Corey belted out a melody in my living room, I knew he had something special. A talent like his shouldn't just be spent singing Luther Vandross covers at block parties. I really believed he could make it big. I wanted it so badly for him that Corey started to want it for himself.

"You gotta get me on stage, Miss Diane," he'd say. "I just wanna sing."

And I did. I called in every favor I could and got him on every stage in the area. He'd sing his heart out wherever he was. His smooth R&B baritone still made me melt each time I heard it. So when I just happened to meet a music producer, I knew I had to get Corey in front of him. He wasn't with a big label, but he had the connections to give Corey a real shot at a singing career.

"Aw, man, Miss Diane," Corey said when I told him. He grinned and jittered like a kid waiting for Christmas morning. "Just wait till I sing for this dude. I'm gonna show him what I can do."

I sat back and smiled as he practiced his songs over and over again in my little studio. He and Craig had written this slow jam I loved called "Please Baby Please." He was going to sing it for the producer, along with some covers. Other kids popped their heads in, telling him a song they thought he should sing or yelling, "That sounds real good!" I closed my eyes, listening to him practice a phrase or a note until it was spot on. *This boy is going places*, I thought.

I figured Corey would show up early the day we had an appointment with the producer. I made sure the DeVille had plenty of gas in the tank so I didn't have to stop on our way. I didn't want Corey to worry about being late. I sat down in a folding chair and waited. Minutes came and went with no sign of Corey.

When our appointment was only fifteen minutes away, I got worried. *It's not like Corey not to show up*, I thought. *He wants this. He's ready. He's been practicing. The only way he wouldn't be here is if something happened to him.*

I called everybody who I thought might know where he was. Jamal. DaJuan. I was *this close* to calling his mom, but since I knew she had health problems, I didn't want to worry her. Aisha eventually came home and panicked right along with me. All I could think was he was shot somewhere, lying on the ground, all alone. It was way past time for our appointment when I had to call the producer and tell him we weren't going to make it.

Finally, when I was going crazy with worry, Aisha got ahold of Corey's cousin, Malcom. I leaned up next to her so I could hear what he had to say. "Oh, he good, he good," I heard Malcom say. "He'll be over there later."

I put my hand on my chest and heaved a big sigh of relief. "Oh, thank God," I said, hugging Aisha.

That's when it hit me. If Corey was alright, that meant he'd just stood up this producer. *If the gangs didn't kill Corey, I just might have to finish the job.*

I was ready to pounce when Corey strolled into my house that evening like nothing had happened.

"Corey! Where have you been?" I shouted. "You had us all worried sick. Why didn't you show up? Don't you wanna do something with your life? Do you want to be a singer or not?"

Corey shook his head and sighed. "Miss Diane, I had to ride."

"What?" I stared at him, blinking with disbelief. "What you mean, you had to ride?"

"Malcom's crew is into it with that gang up the block." Corey shrugged. "They had to ride over to Sean's house. They said it was time to go. When they ride, I have to ride."

I threw my hands up and walked across the living room floor. The other kids hushed their conversations as they listened. "I don't understand. Why would you sit in the car and watch them shoot up Sean's house? He's your best friend."

He shrugged again. "Yeah, but Malcom is family."

My head ached as I listened to what this boy thought was a good reason for throwing away an opportunity and participating in a drive-by shooting all in the same afternoon. I'd spent the last three years mentoring this boy, encouraging him, and acting like some kind of agent. I'd done everything I could think of to get him straightened out. And I still couldn't get him away from the gangs, even though he wasn't a member.

*God, what am I supposed to do?* I prayed that night as I paced my bedroom floor. *These kids are facing demons that I can't beat. I've been fighting for three years, and it feels like I'm getting nowhere.*

I was so desperate to help Corey I even picked up the phone and called his mom after all. I begged her to talk to him and let him know that he has a real talent and that what he's trying to do is more important than these streets.

I also called the producer again. He wasn't exactly thrilled to talk to the woman who had stood him up just a few days earlier. But I begged for another chance. Literally, I would have crawled on my hands and knees if I was in front of him. Eventually, he said, "Okay. I really want to hear this kid."

I couldn't wait to tell Corey he had another chance. This time the producer would come to my house.

"Don't you screw this up," I warned him. "You better be there fifteen minutes early. You gotta show up."

Corey promised he would be there. Just like last time, he practiced the same songs and seemed excited to get in front of the producer.

But once again, the appointment came and went. Corey didn't show. This producer, bless his heart, waited a solid two hours just in case Corey was running late. Finally, I looked at my watch and sighed. "I give up," I told him.

The producer just shook his head. "Sometimes you can't help these kids when they don't want to help themselves," he said. I just held my head in my hands, not sure whether I was more heartsick than I was angry.

Corey stopped by my house that evening to talk with me. This time, he said, his mom wouldn't let him come. She was convinced I was trying to use him to get rich, he told me. He said she wanted to help him herself.

I sank into a metal folding chair. My legs wouldn't hold me anymore. I wanted to scream or throw something. All I wanted to do was help this boy, and now even his own mama was working against me. *I really am on my own*, I thought. *Nobody's going to help me help him. Not even his family.*

And yet, I couldn't give up on him. Something inside me kept saying maybe next time he'll get it. You never know what's going to spark a change in a kid. These boys and girls had lived in these circumstances long before I invited them into my living room. Their families still live that way. Their lives weren't going to change overnight or even in three years. I should know that better than anyone.

I thought of myself at twenty-seven years old, sitting next to my mama, sobbing. My first husband had left me, I didn't have a job, and I had no idea how I was supposed to be the mom I needed to be for six kids. She suggested I let my auntie take the girls for a while until I got back on my feet. Let me tell you, that was a blow. But she was right. It wasn't until I met James a few years later that my life started to change. If I hadn't gotten it together until I was in my thirties, why would I expect these kids to turn around right away? If I wanted to help them, I had to play the long game.

So I kept trying. I kept meeting other producers, getting Corey into more rooms with important people. Sometimes he showed up. Sometimes he messed up. But I couldn't give up on him. I could never give up on a kid.

A lot of people couldn't understand it. I'd learned not to read the comments when a newspaper or TV station ran a story about me. Everybody said I was crazy for letting these gangbangers in my house. "I wonder what's gonna happen when she winds up dead," they'd say. Some people even called me wanting to know if I was some kind of gang mother.

I knew what that really meant. These people thought every black kid was a gangbanger and a thug, somebody to avoid if they saw them on the street. The do-gooders out there all claimed to want to help the inner-city, at-risk kids. But really, they only wanted to help the "good kids." The ones who didn't make them nervous.

*If everybody could just meet these kids and talk to them, I know I could change their minds*, I thought. I was out there begging anybody and everybody to volunteer, come to my house, spend some time with the kids from my neighborhood. Once, early on, a white couple who had seen me on TV sent me money and reached out to say they supported what I was doing. When they were planning to visit Chicago, the wife contacted me to say they wanted to stop by and see the kids. Finally, somebody was going to see that these kids were worth saving, that their lives mattered.

A couple days before the visit, my phone rang. It was the woman who'd sent me the donation. "What's a good time for us to visit? You know, before dark?" she asked. "And are the police usually around?"

*Whoa, hey now*, I thought. *This is my home. This is where I live. And you're scared to even step foot here?*

That couple never showed. No explanation. I never heard from them again.

This was constant. Every day I was out there practically begging people to help me. I needed their time, I needed their money, I needed them to just show me that they cared about these kids. I was putting myself out there like I was some kind of charity case begging for scraps. It felt humiliating, but I didn't see any way around it. I needed help. Over and over, people would smile and nod and tell me they'd donate or that they'd stop by my house to help mentor the young boys. Most of the time they were lying. They never came through. Their lies hurt worse than a flat-out rejection. At least the people who told me no were honest.

I'm not sure what happened on the day that the burden became just too much. One minute I was sitting in the dining room, talking to James and thinking about what I'd do with the KOB kids that week. Maybe I was wishing I had volunteers to help me besides James. Maybe I was disappointed I didn't have the money to take the kids on a little day trip that weekend. Whatever it was, my eyes filled with tears.

*I'm all alone*, I thought. *Nobody wants to help me. Nobody's ever going to help me. Nobody gets what I'm doing, and they don't want to help these kids.*

The tears overflowed from my eyes and streamed down my cheeks. I tried to wipe them away, but they wouldn't stop. Sobs formed in the back of my throat, and I sniffled as I tried to choke them back.

"What's wrong?" James asked. I didn't answer. I just made a beeline for the bathroom.

I locked the door behind me and let everything out. This was no pretty, dainty cry. This was a snot-flying, wailing-like-a-two-year-old, ugly cry. I didn't care who heard me or what they thought. I gave myself permission to bawl my eyes out, hollering like a kid who'd lost her candy. I was sick of feeling alone. I hated begging. I hated lowering myself like that, only to be rejected time and time again.

*It's too much. You got the wrong woman, Lord. I ain't cut out for this. I can't do it anymore.*

My husband did what any sane man would do. He ran for the hills—or at least, straight to my mama's house. Next thing I knew, my mama was banging on the bathroom door.

"Diane, come on out of there," I heard her call.

I shook my head even though I knew she couldn't see me. "Ma, I can't," I gasped between sobs. "I can't do it no more."

"Do what, honey?"

"Any of it." I took a deep breath. The tears kept coming. "Nobody will help me, Ma. Nobody understands what I'm trying to do. I'm sick of begging for help. I can't do it anymore."

"Diane." My mama's voice was calm. "It's your vision. God gave it to you. He didn't give it to them."

The sobs stopped coming as I listened closer.

"Why are you expecting them to do something?" she went on. "Of course they don't understand it. How could they? God didn't reveal it to them. He revealed it to you."

Her words resonated with me. As much as I didn't want to admit it, my mama was right. Why was I trying to make people do what God had called me to do? They didn't get it. Maybe they never would. But I did.

*You got this*, I felt God telling me. *Just follow Me. Let them catch your vision. Then they'll help you.*

My mom was waiting for me when I finally emerged from the bathroom, my eyes red, my face still dripping with tears and who knows what else. She took one look at me and laughed.

"I swear, Diane, you act just like you did when you were five years old throwing a fit."

I had to laugh too. "I threw a pretty good tantrum there, didn't I?"

Her words didn't take any responsibilities off my plate. They didn't put more money in my pocket or draw more volunteers to my program. But something about my mindset shifted that day. My mama had taught me and my sisters to earn respect. She'd taught us that if you built something to be proud of, your followers would come. I'd been so busy feeling sorry for myself that I'd forgotten that. Maybe they didn't understand what I was doing or why they should help these kids. Instead of begging and pleading for them to change their minds, I had to show them. And the only way I could do that was by doing what I was supposed to do. What God had called me to do.

So I kept on running my program. I kept on holding basketball games on the lot and putting kids on stages to perform. And I invited people to come watch. I invited their parents, local politicians, people from other organizations. "Come hang out with us today," I'd say. "We over here on Michigan." Instead of begging them to come help us, I invited them to come be part of KOB. We had it going on.

And it worked. Before I knew it, word had spread throughout the community about KOB. Our name was on the lips of people I'd never heard of. People were giving us credit for things we hadn't even done. Instead of me calling people, I had new volunteers calling me asking if they could please help out.

All this time, I'd been begging God to send me help. But the whole time, He wanted me to look inward. I didn't need to change my circumstances. I needed to change myself.

# Headstones

Something was off from the moment Aisha pushed open the front door. I was in the kitchen fixing sandwiches and gathering up bags of chips and juice bottles, getting ready to head across the street. It was a warm day—May 10, 2007. A perfect day for an evening of basketball. Kids were still in school, and it was one of those rare moments when even the kids who didn't go to school had left to check in with their parents or meet up with their friends, and the house was completely empty. Aisha usually burst through the door around this time, throwing down her backpack and barging into the kitchen announcing she needed a snack before telling me all about which girl said what to her that day. Aisha always had something to say.

But today, she was quiet. All I could hear was a sniffle here and there.

"Aisha, what's going on?" I asked, looking up at my daughter.

She plopped down in the one comfy chair we had left in our living room and held her head in her hands. She stared at me, her mouth unable to form the words, before she finally spoke. "Blair was killed."

I felt my stomach flip-flop with those three words. I'd only met Blair a time or two. Back when Aisha was a freshman, the two of them went to school together, and I got to know Blair's father, Ron Holt. Ron was a police officer, and I always deeply respected him. I knew his son was a sweet, smart kid with light skin and cornrows who loved to rap and write his own lyrics. He was an honor-roll student on his way up. He wasn't going to get stuck in the South Side, wasting his life gangbanging for some clique. This kid was going places. For a moment, I thought there had to be some mistake.

"What?" I sputtered. "*Blair* Blair? That boy?"

"Mooooom!" Aisha wailed. Her voice broke into a scream unlike anything I'd heard since she was a toddler. It was a scream of grief, a scream of fear that she could be next, a scream of anger that somebody like Blair, somebody who did all the right things, could have their life cut off at sixteen.

Watching my baby scream like that made me scream right along with her. My mama instincts kicked in as I scooped her up in the chair and sat with her, holding her and stroking her hair as we cried together.

Kids showed up one by one as we sobbed in the living room. Nobody asked why we were crying. By now, everybody knew. It was all over the news that Blair had been on a city bus, riding to his after-school job at his grandma's store, when a fourteen-year-old with a grudge and a gun boarded the bus. Bullets flew as this boy pulled the trigger over and over again. Blair, the son of a police officer, whose mother was a firefighter, instantly dove in front of the girl seated next to him and pushed her out of the way. The girl survived. Blair did not.

Shootings aren't uncommon on the South Side. Kids are murdered so frequently that half the time, it doesn't even make the news. Blair wasn't even the first kid close to Aisha to be killed. But Blair's story was different. Nobody could say, "Oh, if he hadn't been running around gangbanging, he wouldn't have got killed." Nobody could think to themselves, "Well, that would never happen to me. I'd never be in that situation." Blair was just a good kid who got on the wrong bus at the wrong time. It could happen to anybody, whether they chose the right path in life or not.

Even the kids who didn't know Blair were uneasy that night. They wanted to know why God would let something like this happen. That was a question I couldn't answer. Other kids asked why they should do the right thing when their lives could be taken anyway. If I wasn't talking to a kid, I was busy on the phone listening to somebody ask if I was watching the news or if I saw the story on this or that channel. Some channels even showed a clip from the bus's videotape of the shooter walking onto the bus, just before he opened fire.

The room spun around me as I fielded questions. It was like I was watching myself sitting in my crowded living room. I was still in shock. I'd been to so many funerals since I'd started KOB. I'd seen too many mamas crying over caskets. I was so tired of accepting as a fact of life that some kids aren't going to live to see their twenties. Most of these kids didn't show they were upset when they told me about a friend or cousin who was shot. Even if they were hurting, they stuffed it down. They had to just to survive, to keep living in this neighborhood knowing they took their lives in their hands every time they stepped out the front door. Now here we were, talking about Blair's funeral. Blair, who should have been studying for finals, writing rap lyrics, picking out colleges. It was wrong. It was all wrong.

Just about everybody I'd ever met in the Chicago nonprofit world called me the next day. "We gotta march," they said. "Let's have a rally." I just wasn't feeling it. Not this time.

Normally, I was all for a march or rally. I'd throw on my KOB T-shirt, write "Save Our Teens" on a poster board, and head downtown. Hundreds of people would march up and down the sidewalks and offer up our thoughts and prayers. Politicians would take photos with us, and we'd see our pictures in the paper the next day. Then we'd all go home feeling better about ourselves for doing something. I probably marched or went to a rally at least once a week. Somebody was always having one, and I was so new to the nonprofit world that I felt I always needed to show my face at them.

But as my phone rang off the hook that day, I realized all those marches and rallies were nothing but talk. We said the same old things, took the same old photos, and nothing ever changed. These marches weren't helping our communities. They weren't keeping our young people alive. I imagined God listening to our prayers and shaking His head. I pictured Him saying, "I appreciate the prayers, but could y'all get out there and do something?" God put us on this earth to do something, to help each other. Marching down a street holding up a sign seemed like a lazy person's answer. It was all for the media. When I thought about marching for Blair's death, these marches felt sick and twisted, like in some way they were glorifying the killing of young people.

"Well, what else do you want everybody to do?" James asked me as I ranted to him that night about yet another planned march.

I threw my hands in the air as I paced around the bedroom. "I don't know. Something bolder."

"Bolder?" James shook his head. "What else are they supposed to do?"

"Go with me to city hall. Camp out and don't eat for three days until the mayor comes out and says, 'What do you all want?'"

"And what do you want?"

I sat down on the bed and rubbed my temples with my fingers. My thoughts were spinning so fast my head hurt. "I want them to invest in our neighborhood. These kids don't have jobs. They don't have nothing to do. This place looks like a war zone. And they wonder why they're all shooting each other."

James shook his head. "Diane, ain't nobody gonna open a business here when they can't even put a clerk behind a desk without bulletproof glass."

"That's the catch-22, isn't it?" I looked at James with despair. "The violence ain't gonna leave until the businesses come."

He nodded. Roseland had all but been abandoned. Like our community didn't matter. Like our young people didn't matter. It was hard not to feel as though life might be different if our faces were white.

"So what are you gonna do?" he finally asked.

"We gon' do our own thing." The words were out of my mouth before I even had a plan. But I went with it. "I'll call up the reporters and tell them we'll be over here on Michigan if they want to see how the kids feel about all this violence."

The day before Blair's funeral, I pulled out my list of about twenty media outlets and called every single one of them. I didn't have a big event planned. The kids didn't even know I'd invited the media, and I had no idea what they would say. I just told the reporters that KOB kids would be talking about Blair's death and how they felt about living with this violence. Some of them didn't answer, but a few said they'd try to make it. That was enough for me.

As kids shuffled into my house, I told them to spread the word to their friends about the reporters coming and asked if they could talk about how they felt. I wasn't surprised when most of them said yes. They were sad. They were serious. And they wanted to talk about it.

By the time the media showed up, we had a little amp and microphone set up in the vacant lot across the street for anybody who wanted to speak. For one day, we wouldn't unchain the basketball hoop from my porch and roll it across the street. The only sound was the kids' solemn voices.

Reporters listened as the kids talked about being terrified to walk to school, about the gangs that ruled their streets, about wondering if they would live long enough to graduate from high school. A few of them read poems from notebook paper, their voices shaking. Some rapped their emotions. My daughter even sang "C'mon, Young People." Tears poured down my cheeks as Aisha's soaring voice sang the words I'd written years before, words that seemed truer today than they had four years earlier. She gripped the microphone and closed her eyes, swaying as she crooned the chorus.

C'mon, young people
Let's get it together
This is our situation
We're killing each other

From the first day I invited Aisha's friends into my living room, KOB was my calling, my passion, my purpose, which God had given me. Now, as I looked around at the boys and girls at that press conference, I realized this was literally a life-and-death situation. Any one of them, even my own daughter, could end up like Blair if I didn't do something. Whether a kid was a gang leader or a student council president, every single one of them mattered. Somebody loved them, worried about them, changed their diapers when they were babies. All of them were worth saving. And all of them were worth remembering. The urgency that had always filled me grew into an all-out frenzy as I watched my kids mourn in the parking lot. *I'm gonna save these kids*, I thought. *I'll meet with every single new kid. I'll find out where they're coming from and why they're acting the way they do. I'll find out why they're asking for help. I gotta do what it takes to keep them alive.*

The dust had settled about a week later when James and I pushed an orange cart down the Home Depot aisle looking for paint to fix up some chairs. Like any other trip, we wound up walking up and down the aisles, browsing the tools and plants lining the shelves, even though we didn't need them. That's when I noticed the terra-cotta garden pavers. Their flat sides slanted out into a curve, so that one end of rough stone was wider than the other.

I barely glanced at those pavers for more than a second before we were down the aisle, on to the next thing we didn't need. I'd seen those stones a thousand times in friends' backyards and gardens and never thought twice about them. But this time, something about them stuck in my head. They reminded me of something I couldn't quite place.

A few minutes later, it hit me.

"James, let's go back to those stones," I said, tugging at his arm.

James hadn't noticed them. "What stones?"

"The ones over there in that aisle. The ones that look like little headstones."

"Diane, we all the way over here," James fussed. "Now you wanna walk all the way back?"

I pushed the cart away from him. "Well, I'ma walk over there," I said, knowing he'd follow.

James stood behind me as I studied those stones. Minutes ticked by as I looked at them, an idea forming in my head. I thought of all the young people gunned down in the streets, on their porches, on buses. I thought of the boys who weren't like Blair, who didn't make good choices, who didn't have their deaths commemorated with marches and rallies, whose names weren't even deemed worthy of the newspaper's police blotter. *How many young people are we going to lose before somebody stands up and does something?* I thought.

James looked around impatiently, waiting for me to speak. Finally, I turned to him.

"I just want to shock the community," I said.

"What?" he asked.

I looked at the price below the stones—$1.37. I opened my wallet to see how much was inside. "I think I got enough for thirty stones."

"Thirty?" James spat out. "What you gonna do with thirty stones?"

I waved off his question. Mostly because I didn't know the answer yet. I was still figuring that part out. "Just help me load the cart."

James fussed about lifting those heavy stones into the trunk and how he didn't want to drag them out of the car. I was too lost in thought to tell him to hush.

What was I going to do with those stones anyway? I didn't have a plan. All I had was a concept. For the last four years, I'd spent every waking moment trying to help kids stay in school, get their grades up, stay away from gangs. But no matter what I did, there were still kids out there dying every day. I'd done nothing to remember them. And now I had these garden pavers that reminded me of headstones.

We pulled in front of our house and parked in my usual spot. When we'd unloaded the pavers, I stood back and stared at the pile with my arms crossed, frowning. I had a vision now. A vision of Blair's name and age written on a headstone. *Ain't nobody gonna forget Blair,* I thought. *Not if I can help it. Not Blair or no other kid who loses their life.*

My eyes drifted to a woodpile in the corner of the lot. James had planned to build a bench with it for our basketball games. Now I couldn't help thinking it might be put to better use.

I looked up at James. "Could you build me something to put the stones on?"

"Build what?" He shook his head as his voice grew loud. "You just asked me to build a bench with all that wood. Now you want me to build something else, but you can't even tell me what it is?"

But before he could say another word, he caught a glimpse of my face and stopped. He could tell this was no harebrained idea. This was serious.

"I want to do this for Blair," I said. "Please?"

James was quiet as he hauled out his toolbox and set up sawhorses. Before long he was hammering and sawing away. By now, I had kids sauntering up to my porch and giving James the side-eye.

"What you gonna do with all those stones, Miss Diane?" Jamal asked.

I wasn't quite ready to explain yet. I gathered everybody up on the porch and took out my notebook and pen. "Can y'all tell me who's been killed recently?"

The boys and girls were silent for a moment before somebody hollered the first name. Then another. And another. I scratched my pen across the paper, hurrying to keep up with their growing list.

I enlisted everybody to gather up any spray-paint cans they could find and make a sign with one of the boards James wasn't using. Then I called up the guy who airbrushed our KOB T-shirts to spray names on the stones—their surface was too slick for even the ink of a Sharpie to stick.

By the end of the evening, the kids and I sat somberly on my porch as we took in our work. Across the street, in front of the lot where we played basketball, stood a small wooden pyramid holding seven stones. "Blair Holt, 16," was scrawled in black across the center stone. The big plywood board was now covered in brightly colored spray paint with the words "Save a teen. Do something. How many more?" My question was for everybody. The neighborhood. The city. State and federal officials. I wanted them to look at this memorial and seriously ask themselves how many more of our young people had to die before they invested in our community and did something.

All afternoon, the kids had buzzed with excitement. They bragged about their spray-painting skills and said they couldn't wait for everybody to see our work. But now, as they stared at headstones, at the sign screaming out my plea, they were silent. Nobody moved.

A deep sense of peace washed over me as I patted Aisha's knee and gazed at the memorial. I had done what I was supposed to do. That nagging sense of urgency I'd felt all afternoon gave way to overwhelming calm as the sun faded in the sky. *Now they won't be forgotten*, I thought. *Everybody's gonna know these kids mattered.*

"You think anybody's family is gonna mind that we used their kid's name?" Aisha asked.

My stomach lurched. The thought had not occurred to me the entire time we'd painted and placed stones. My only focus was on remembering these kids. But what if their parents didn't like it? What if they got mad and demanded I take the stones down?

"I guess we'll just have to see," I said.

I couldn't avoid marching forever. About a month after Blair's death, when somebody invited me to a march with Mayor Richard Daley, I felt the Lord telling me to get over myself and go.

Chicago is always hot in the summer, and that sweltering June day was no exception. Add to that the fact that I was packed in with about four hundred people, and it was downright roasting. I stayed near the back of the crowd as we marched three blocks toward my house on Michigan. Mayor Daley was in the front with all the pastors and my alderman.

When we got to the north side of the lot by my house, Mayor Daley headed across the street to the corner gas station. I don't know if that was on the route, but since the mayor went, everybody followed him. Somehow I drifted closer to the front, close enough to hear the alderman telling the mayor about how the city had cleared trees from the lot. You could see the back of the memorial right from where we stood.

*This is my moment*, I thought. *I gotta get the mayor to see this.*

I pushed and shoved my way over to the mayor until suddenly I was right next to him. Without thinking, I grabbed the mayor's hand. Of course, he snatched it back. I'm sure he was thinking, "This lady is crazy."

"No, no," I said, holding my hands up to show I meant him no harm. "I'm Diane Latiker. I have an organization over here. With all due respect, Mayor, I just want you to see something."

He looked at me skeptically as he let me take his hand—lightly this time. The whole crowd followed us as he walked with me to our little pyramid memorial.

Mayor Daley was quiet as he stood with his arms crossed, his intimidating figure hunched down small, as if he were really studying these stones.

"These are names of young people killed by violence," I said quietly. "This shouldn't be happening."

I could see my alderman's face turning red with fury. I wondered if maybe I'd made a mistake. Then I looked at Mayor Daley. To my surprise, tears were rolling down his cheeks.

When the reporters stuck their microphones in his face, the mayor cleared his throat and smoothed his tie before he turned to face the crowd and did exactly what I'd hoped he would do. He talked about the violence.

I did not have this big plan for a growing memorial. I didn't think about what we'd do as we ran out of space for more stones. But in a neighborhood like ours, there were always more names to add, more young people whose lives were stolen. Before long, I had to ask James to rebuild the memorial to make space for more stones. And when we ran out of space again, I asked him to make it even bigger. And bigger. My kids took their cans of spray paint and created a mural of the city skyline, with our KOB logo in the middle of Lake Michigan. Along the bottom, my plea shouted out to the neighborhood in capital letters: "SAVE A TEEN. DO SOMETHING."

Nearly every day, I'd write down a name as I heard about a murder on the news or from somebody in KOB. When I got an extra dollar or two, I drove out to Home Depot to buy more stones. There were never enough. I always had more names than I had stones and space.

As the years went by, our little seven-stone pyramid ballooned into a full-blown memorial with nearly eight hundred stones. James built a shelter with row after row of wire racks to hold the same little stone pavers. Even then, I was still four hundred names behind.

My little memorial became a place of healing for families. I'd come outside to find a father holding his son's memorial stone, or a mother on her knees weeping. Once, when I heard somebody crying, I looked out my window and saw a boy's mama wailing, clutching a stone to her heart. I recognized her right away. Her boy was in my program and was only fifteen when he got shot walking across the street holding a box of Church's Chicken. I could feel the Lord telling me not to leave her over there by herself.

I walked across the street and gently laid my hand on her shoulder. She turned and laid her head on my shoulder, screaming her baby's name. My heart ached as she sobbed and sobbed, her tears soaking through my T-shirt.

*God, can You ease her pain just a little?* I prayed. *Even just the tiniest bit.* My prayers were all I had to offer. The sound of her cries replayed in my mind like a record.

I wished her son's name would be the last one I added to the memorial. But it wasn't. Not by a long shot.

# CHAPTER TEN

# When the Lord Takes You Down a Peg

Four years into running KOB, something inside my brain shifted. I had long since stopped apologizing as I asked for donations, applied for grants, and recruited volunteers. I wasn't out hitting the streets begging for scraps anymore. I just told everybody, "We over here on Michigan," and waited for them to come.

And they did. Money from donors kept us supplied with new basketballs, matching T-shirts, and sandwiches and chips. Volunteers helped me keep an eye on the dozens of teenagers filling my house every day. And after countless rejection letters, I finally got a state grant. My chest puffed out a little. My head swelled so big it's a wonder it fit through the doorway.

It didn't help that people in Chicago knew who I was now. When people said "Diane Latiker," everybody in the nonprofit community, and sometimes beyond, knew that meant Kids Off the Block. After more than four years of showing up to every organization's march and rally, I started thinking maybe I was something too. Maybe I could command the same kind of attention as CeaseFire and Magic. Maybe if I hosted my own event, everybody would show up just like they did for these organizations I'd looked up to since I first started KOB.

I spent a little too much time listening to myself instead of listening to the Lord. If I'd listened to Him, I would have heard Him warning me that pride goes before a fall. But I was so sure I was running the next big organization that I'm not sure I would have listened.

It all started with a boy named Robert. He was just thirteen years old, and his only mistake was winning a game of dice against a couple of older boys about two blocks from me. Thirty minutes after those boys left, they went back and shot him in the street, right in front of his house.

Chicago went through its usual outrage cycle. Everybody wanted to march and rally. My phone rang off the hook with calls from the same old people, inviting me to this event and that. This time, though, an idea came to me.

"I'm gonna host my own march," I told the kids. "You guys show up with signs. I'll invite the media and all them other groups to come with us."

The kids all nodded. "Yeah, Miss Diane, we be there," a few of them said.

I was confident as I took out my list of twenty reporters and worked the phones, talking with everybody who answered and leaving messages for everybody who didn't. I called up every nonprofit leader I knew and invited them to my march.

Some of them said they were hosting their own events. Some of them said they might try to come.

The kids and I canvassed the neighborhood, knocking on doors, inviting everybody we saw, and plastering every blank surface with flyers. At night, I took out a notebook and pen and mapped out my route, making sure we'd hit the busiest streets in Roseland for the most exposure.

That Saturday, the morning of the march, I woke up and opened the blinds, peeking out the window and praying for clear skies. Even a few drops of rain could be enough to keep crowds and reporters from braving the streets. Sunlight streamed through the glass. Only a few fluffy clouds dotted the blue sky. *It's gonna be a good day*, I thought.

I washed my face and pulled on my favorite T-shirt airbrushed with the KOB logo before I pulled my braids into an updo. James and I puttered around the house for a few hours, attempting to put everything back in order after a week of kids tearing the place apart. Then, when the march was a half hour away, I sat on my front porch and waited.

I don't run programming on Saturdays, but that doesn't stop a few kids from coming by here and there. Today, though, the street was quiet. A few cars drove by but didn't park nearby. Neighbors walked right by my house. I checked my watch. The march was supposed to start in five minutes, and I was all alone. My heart sank as I considered for the first time the very real possibility that nobody, not even my KOB kids, were coming.

*They couldn't even show up for me?* I thought, my cheeks burning. *After all I do for them? After all those marches and rallies I went to?*

Ten minutes later, I saw Juan, one of my KOB kids, swaggering up the street, smiling broadly, a poster board tucked under his arm. His smile faded as he looked around and realized he was the only one there.

"Where everybody else at, Miss Diane?" he asked.

I shook my head. It didn't matter how embarrassed or disappointed I felt, I refused to let this boy know it.

"Don't worry about everybody else," I said firmly. "We gonna march."

I held my head high as I walked down the steps and onto the sidewalk. Juan shrugged and held up his poster board scrawled with the words "Stop the Violence." Side by side, we marched down Michigan to State Street, over to the side block on 117th, and all the way over to Lafayette, past the burned-out houses and buildings marked with red *X*s, past the boarded-up windows, and under the cameras on lampposts. I saw people on their porches snickering as we turned around and walked down to LaSalle before heading up Perry, passing the block where Robert was killed.

A few times, Juan trailed behind, his whole demeanor pleading, "Do we really have to keep doing this?" I kept my resolve. I said I was going to march, and I was going to do it with or without a big crowd.

Cars honked at us as we turned back up Michigan and down 115th to end our march at the lot. I had planned to say a few words in front of the memorial. Now that was pointless.

Juan put down his sign. "That it, Miss Diane?" he asked.

I sighed. It was the first time I allowed myself to show any sign of frustration or disappointment. I'd held it together the whole march, but I was starting to lose steam. "That's it. You can go." I put my hand on his shoulder and gave him a half-smile. "Thanks for showing up."

"Why didn't nobody else come?" he asked innocently.

I shrugged. "I honestly have no idea."

I stood in front of the memorial and shaded my eyes, watching Juan walk toward his house to make sure he made it safely. Once again, I was all alone, and I sure felt it. I thought of all the kids who'd said they'd march with me, all the times I'd faithfully shown up for marches and rallies even when I could have been doing something more exciting with my time. Nobody but Juan could be bothered to show up for me, and that stung. I felt hurt, like I didn't matter to anybody else as much as they mattered to me. I wished I'd chosen a less visible route.

My ego deflated as I trudged across the street to my house. My head was back to its normal size now.

*I never told you to march*, I could feel the Lord telling me. *I never told you that you had it going on. None of this is about you. This has always been about Me.*

If anybody had asked me, I would have sworn that I listened to God in that moment. I prayed for forgiveness. I promised to listen and give Him the glory. But deep down, some part of me still longed for approval. Sure, God should get credit for all of it, but I could use a few pats on the back now and then. Was that really so bad? I didn't think so at the time. But God must not have agreed. He wasn't done humbling me yet.

I was out on the porch with James one May morning when I saw a nice-looking light-skinned man heading down the sidewalk. He stuck out like a sore thumb on my street, with his neatly ironed collared shirt. A notebook stuck out of the back pocket of his jeans.

"That must be Don Terry," I whispered to James.

Don was a reporter with the *Chicago Tribune*, and he'd called me a few days earlier asking to write an article about me and

KOB. This was no typical article though. He wanted to follow me for two weeks and write a big feature for the last issue of the *Chicago Tribune* magazine.

I was giddy when I told James, and I warned the kids that he was coming. It wasn't exactly my first time in the media or even my first article in the *Tribune*. But the thought of having a well-respected man like Don Terry tell our story excited me. Maybe people would finally understand what I was doing. I was no fool. I knew some of the other nonprofit leaders whispered about me when I wasn't around. They didn't like that I allowed gang members to hang out in my living room. I just knew Don would be on my side, that he'd write the perfect article and win everybody else over to my side too.

James and I shook Don's hand as he introduced us to the photographer who would take our pictures.

"I want you to pretend I'm not here," he explained to us. "I'll sit back and take notes, and I might ask you a few questions when you have a moment. I'll be your shadow. Just keep doing what you're doing."

I nodded to James, who was still munching on his bowl of cereal. I wondered what I'd gotten myself into. I wasn't sure how I felt about somebody watching my every move for the next two weeks. What if this reporter didn't like what we were doing or got the wrong idea? What if this article ripped me to shreds? I hoped I wouldn't say anything stupid.

"We about to head across the street if y'all want to join us. The kids are playing basketball."

The words were barely out of my mouth when we heard somebody scream. We jerked up our heads to look out the window. Corey was already across the street with Joe, who was new to KOB, and a few new kids. Even from my living room, I could see fear on Corey's face.

"Uh-oh," I said.

Before anybody could say a word, I threw open the front door and ran as fast as my feet could carry me to the lot across the street.

"Miss Diane's coming!" I heard somebody yell.

James was panting behind me, still carrying that bowl of cereal. There was Joe with a rock the size of a boulder in his hand, still screaming at Corey. Joe was shorter than Corey and half his weight, but he waved that rock around like he was the Hulk, his body twisting with rage. Corey wasn't backing down, his fists up, still cursing at Joe and insulting the boy's mother.

For a moment, I forgot all about Don Terry. I didn't think about the photographer snapping pictures. My focus was on one thought—keeping these boys alive. *I can't have nobody getting hurt on my watch*, I thought frantically. *It's never happened before. Today ain't gonna be the day.*

I jumped in front of Corey and held my arms out. Corey was several inches taller than me, but I felt invincible. "Stop it. Stop it now."

"You ain't gonna do nothing!" Corey shouted, still taunting Joe. "You a punk."

Joe lunged at Corey, his eyes flashing, his arm cocked behind him like a slingshot ready to fling the rock. "I ain't no punk!" he screamed.

"Stop!" I hollered at the top of my lungs. "Put the rock down. Now!"

I grabbed Joe's wrists, squeezing them until he dropped the rock. *I can't hold him long*, I thought as he struggled under my grip. Before I could stop him, he wriggled away from me and charged Corey. I screamed at him to stop as he flew off the asphalt and flung his fist into Corey's face.

I didn't see Joe's brother Stanley sneak up behind us and grab the rock his brother had dropped. Somebody yelled for us to duck just in time. The rock sailed past Corey, hitting the back fence with a sickening smack.

My heart pounded with fury as I fought back a scream. *He did not just do that with me standing right there.*

"Give me my phone," I yelled to my husband, still standing there with his bowl of cereal. "I'm calling the police."

James shook his head as he handed me my phone and scowled at the boys. "Y'all oughtta be ashamed of yourselves!" he yelled. "All Diane do for y'all, and y'all acting like this?"

I dressed all three of them up and down as I held up my phone, ready to call the police at a moment's notice. "We don't play like this over here," I shouted. "Y'all know better. I'm not gonna keep risking my life to save y'all if y'all keep acting like this. You think I won't call the police? Think again. You wanna go to jail, you throw that rock again."

I waited for somebody to make a move. Moments later, it was like nothing had ever happened. Somebody picked up the basketball. The three boys who were ready to kill one another just a few minutes earlier were laughing and passing the ball.

Don Terry was there the whole time, scribbling notes in his book. *He must think I'm over here working with a bunch of thugs*, I thought, dreading his questions. I walked over to him, bracing myself for the worst.

But instead, Don was curious. "Now, why was Corey saying that to Joe?" he asked. "What happened to his mom?"

I relaxed as I explained to him that Joe's mama was addicted to drugs and that Joe was especially sensitive to any insult that involved her. We were still talking as we walked back to the house.

Hours passed. Don gathered the kids together to explain who he was and what he was doing. He spoke with James, Aisha, a group of boys, anybody who made time for him. And he was back again the next day and the next.

Don wasn't kidding about being my shadow. He followed me everywhere. He was there when I visited Curtis Elementary School for a basketball program, waving to kids as they tugged on my sleeve to tell me who they had a crush on or who won the soccer game that night. He was there when I walked the block, saying hello to neighbors who called, "Hey, Miss Diane!" from their front porches. He was there, riding in my passenger seat and interviewing me as I drove out to community meetings. I'd hold my breath through the entire meeting, hoping nobody said anything out of line. I'd cringe when somebody made a comment about the white people gentrifying our neighborhoods. *Please don't use that in your article*, I'd think.

At first, I spoke carefully, considering how every word could be taken the wrong way. But as the days passed, I forgot to be nervous. I stopped trying to show everything in a positive light. I allowed myself to get heated in community meetings, only to look over and find Don smiling at me. By the time he shook my hand on the last day, I felt like I was saying goodbye to my best friend.

"I'll bring you a copy of the magazine as soon as it runs," he promised me.

I barely slept those few weeks before the article was printed. I lay awake going over every word I'd said, wondering what the kids might have told him. I thought he was on my side. I thought he understood me. But what if I was wrong?

James sighed and rolled his eyes as I brought it up again and again. My kids didn't even want to come over for dinner, they were so sick of hearing about it. "Just pray about it, Mama," they'd say, growing less and less tolerant with each conversation. "It's all gonna be alright. You didn't do anything wrong."

"But what if, in his eyes, I did?" I asked every time.

One day I came home to Don on my front porch with three magazines tucked under his arm. I could see a photo of three KOB kids—Rayshawn, Juan, and Tetey—on the front cover, standing in the alley across the street.

"It printed?" I asked, using every ounce of restraint I had to stop myself from snatching it out of his hand.

"It printed," he said, setting the magazines on the table.

I thanked him for coming out and interviewing me, the whole time glancing nervously at the magazines and wishing he would leave so I could read it. When I was finally alone, I sank into a dining room chair and opened the glossy cover, turning the slick pages until I saw a picture of me. The only word I could say the entire time I read was, "Wow."

Don had written the most beautiful article I'd ever read. He truly understood what I was trying to do and what I was up against in this neighborhood. That little incident with Corey and Joe framed the article. I was blown away. I felt a little extra spring in my step as I went about my programming that night and as I drove to my state grant meeting a few days later.

KOB was one of six organizations to receive a Roseland Safety Net Works grant—it wasn't much, but it was enough to keep us running that summer. One of the requirements was that I attend meetings every week with the organizations that received the grant. We had to talk about summer plans, write reports, plan forums, and go over everything we'd done with the funding. I wouldn't have minded the meetings if it wasn't for Terrell. Terrell was the head of a growing nonprofit and never made it a secret that he didn't like me. It didn't matter what we were talking about, he'd always find a way to make a snippy comment about "those bad KOB kids." I tried to be cordial. I kept my mouth shut. I didn't want to get into it with him in the middle of a meeting. But if he kept going, I'd shut it down with a "Really? You should just stop talking."

Nobody told me they were on his side, but they sure didn't speak up for me. They just sat there, supporting him with their silence, sometimes even nodding their heads. I got to where I couldn't stand being around him, but I didn't have a choice. I had to keep going to those meetings to keep the grant funding.

On this day, I was still on a high from Don's article, but Terrell was doing his best to get me down. We were busy planning an event on Halstead Street when he sneered at me and shook his head.

"Yeah, bring those bad kids from KOB," he scoffed.

Ignoring him didn't do any good. He kept pestering me, wanting to know why I let those thugs in my house.

"Everybody thinks you a gang mother." He was daring me to fight back. "That's why I sent Don Terry over there."

My head snapped up at the mention of Don's name. "What?" In all the hours I'd spent with Don, we never did talk about how he came to write about me in the first place. I felt my stomach churn. I realized he might not have planned to write such a nice article about me.

"Yeah, that's right." Terrell was nodding now, pleased with himself for making me upset. "I called him up. I told him to go over there and investigate what you were really up to."

I felt like somebody had knocked the wind out of me. For five years, I'd dedicated every waking hour to KOB. I mentored kids. I helped them with their homework. I picked them up from school, bailed them out of jail, fixed pallets for them when they slept on my floor. I fed them, clothed them, took them to the barber. Kids who just a few years ago dreamed of nothing but selling drugs were talking about college. They dreamed of life beyond these streets, beyond the gangs, beyond the violence. Maybe I couldn't measure all of that with a few neat statistics, but it was true. And now this man here still didn't think I was the real deal. This man, who worked with me week after week through the grant program.

I wanted to wag my finger and tell Terrell just what I thought of him and his little comments. I wanted to shove Don Terry's article in his face and shout, "Don thinks I'm great. Why don't you?" Instead, I just said, "Wow." I might have muttered a few curse words under my breath. I had to repent of that later.

I was still furious as I paced my bedroom that night. I'd already ranted to James about how Terrell had some nerve disrespecting KOB. When I could tell he was sick of hearing me repeat myself, I called my mom and ranted to her too. Now that I was alone, I let the Lord have it.

*Why can't these people see I'm doing what You asked me to do?* I prayed. *After everything I've done. After how hard I've worked. And this man can't even respect me.*

And there in the stillness, I felt Him speak to me. *But it isn't about you, is it?* I felt him whisper. *It never was. This whole thing is about My glory. Not yours.*

The truth was, I'd been over here thinking I was something else to make a respected reporter like Don Terry want to write about me. I was sick of trying to prove to everyone that I wasn't just some crazy lady trying to convince teenage boys to leave their gangs. The magazine article was my proof to all the haters that I was legitimate. With just a few words, Terrell had ruined it. That man had read the magazine article. It didn't change a thing. He was just mad Don hadn't dug up what he'd wanted him to find. I wasn't upset about KOB being disrespected. I was upset that Don Terry hadn't knocked on my door because I was this big, famous nonprofit director. Once again, my head had gotten a little too big. And the Lord didn't like it.

*You gotta humble yourself*, the Lord whispered to me. *Don't worry about lifting yourself up. You gotta lift Me up.*

I sat on my bed, wiping away the tears. I felt like a little kid who'd just sat through a talking-to from her daddy. *I better listen*, I thought. *'Cause I sure don't want to get chastened again.*

And I did. With every success that's come my way, every victory I've experienced, I pointed the glory right back at God. I wouldn't dare take the credit. I didn't want to find out if He had any other ideas for chastening me.

# Hope and Change

Something different was in the air in 2008. I could feel it. I sensed it in the way people whispered about this young guy with a funny name and big ears. I could see it on their faces, so full of hope even in the middle of an economic train wreck we'd later call the Great Recession. Their voices were hushed with restrained excitement, as if the thing they'd never believed was possible might actually happen. Maybe, just maybe, we might see a black man become president.

I'd heard Barack Obama's name for a couple years by then. I'd even met him once in 2007 at a fundraiser. He was a US senator back then and just starting his run for president. I got to shake his hand on that freezing winter day.

Those of us in Roseland felt a particular claim to Obama as one of our own. Years earlier, he had gotten his start as a community organizer in Roseland's church basements and neighborhood centers. Neighbors remembered fanning themselves in the summer heat, spellbound by this fiery young man speaking so passionately he might as well have been preaching. Everybody said there was something about him, even then. This man was going places, they'd said. And now, here he was, running for president.

Most of the kids in my program didn't pay much attention to the news unless it showed up on BET. I don't normally talk about current events with them beyond who got shot on the block and which gangs are into it these days. But this was different. This was historic. And they needed to hear about it.

The kids, however, weren't so sure when I showed them Obama's picture in the newspaper. DaJuan straight-up rolled his eyes at me like I was crazy.

"Miss Diane, didn't Jesse Jackson run for president too?" he scoffed.

"Well, yeah." I thought back to Reverend Jackson's historic run in the '80s, when I dared to hope he would win. "But this time is different."

Jamal laughed darkly. "They ain't gonna let no black man up in the White House."

I couldn't blame them. I grew up thinking a black president was impossible. Sometimes I allowed myself to dream, to imagine how my life might be different if somebody who looked like me sat in the Oval Office. Somebody who understood my background, my struggles, my needs. But I always shrugged those dreams off quickly. *That's never gonna happen*, I told myself then.

On the South Side, it sure didn't feel like you stood much of a chance getting ahead in the world if you were black. In our eyes, white people held all the power, both in private life and in politics. Being black felt like an automatic disqualifier for any high-level position. I'm often dismissed as an angry black woman for speaking out in a community meeting or am turned down for a grant that inevitably goes to a white person no more qualified than me.

But I couldn't stop hoping. I couldn't stop dreaming that people would change, that the world would get better. And my KOB kids wouldn't give up hoping either, not if I could help it.

"Anything's possible," I told them each time I brought up Obama's name. "Don't count him out."

"Miss Diane, please," they'd protest. I'd have to whip out my pen to shut everybody up.

"Don't be negative," I always said. "You never know."

These conversations went on for months. They kept on going, through the spring primaries and long after Obama clinched the Democratic nomination. "See!" I said gleefully. "You never thought he'd get nominated, and here he is!"

That wasn't enough for them. "Miss Diane, he's from here," Jamal said, shaking his head. "You really think they're gonna let him up in there?"

"Well you're eighteen, and you ain't even registered. How's he supposed to win when none of y'all can vote?"

I wasn't going to let these kids sit on their behinds on Election Day. These kids would get their voting cards if I had to drag them to the registrar's office by their dreads.

I knew where they were coming from. I didn't vote when I was eighteen. Matter of fact, I didn't vote until I was in my thirties. Voting was something other people did. It never felt important to me. Maybe that feeling started when I was a kid. My mom and grandma talked about voting like it was for grown folks. And our polling location was so far from our house that if they had to work or ran short on time, they just didn't vote.

My mom felt her vote was important, but she never pushed it on us kids as something we should do.

By the time I was grown, I didn't give voting a second thought. I was so busy raising my babies and working odd jobs I wasn't going to trek out to my polling place and check a bunch of names on a ballot.

When I was in my early thirties, something changed. I thought about all the time I spent complaining about my city councilman not standing up for the neighborhood, or the state investing in every community but mine. That's when it hit me—I complained about all these people when I didn't even bother to vote against them. Men and women who lived before me fought tirelessly for me to have the right to vote, and I treated that right like trash. The more I thought about it, the more ashamed I felt. So I drove to the city clerk's office and registered. I remember looking at that voter ID card and feeling like I was really somebody.

When the next mayoral election came, I marched out to the polls with my head high and my chest out. I felt grateful, proud, powerful. That's still how I feel when I take a selfie wearing my "I voted" sticker. Everybody knows I'll put up a post on social media with the caption, "I voted, did you?"

My KOB kids weren't so easily convinced. They didn't know how to do it, they didn't want to take the time, they thought it was stupid—this, that, and the other. But when the polls showed Obama with a lead over Senator John McCain, their heads perked up. Their negativity disappeared. They were singing a different tune when I brought up Obama. They talked about him like he was the coming savior of Chicago. The way they talked, you'd think every single one of us would be rich and live in mansions once Obama was president. We sat together dreaming of how Obama would come in and sweep the streets of Chicago and change everything. They wanted to know everything about him—who his wife was, how many kids he had, how long he'd been in politics, you name it. I had to laugh listening to these kids buzzing about somebody they hadn't wanted to hear two words about just a few months earlier.

"Y'all want Obama to be president so bad, you need to get registered," I told them each time his name popped up in conversation. "Y'all need to vote."

Just before the voter registration deadline, I piled every last kid who would be eighteen by Election Day into our two vans. We must have crammed nearly forty in there. James and I had planned to bring them to the city registrar's office, but when we heard about a big voter registration drive going on nearby, we changed course and headed there instead.

These kids' eyes were wide as saucers as they walked into the Operation Push drive at a church on 50th and Drexel. Music blared over the noise of chattering teenagers. I could see Jesse Jackson standing off to the side, taking pictures with kids. Local reporters scribbled in their notebooks and stood holding microphones in front of cameras. The air was electric with excitement, and it was contagious.

Anybody who might have been reluctant to vote was practically jumping up and down to get in line and register. I stood back and watched them, beaming. Some of these kids had been with me from the beginning—Jamal, DaJuan, Senneca, Isiah, Brittany, even Aisha. I'd spent the last five years watching them grow up. These kids had voices. All their lives, they thought their voices didn't matter. Like I thought mine didn't matter. But now, their voices would be heard.

By the time we all loaded back into the vans, every last one of those kids was all amped up with energy. I felt like I was in the car with a bunch of five-year-olds. They wanted to know what their voter card did and if they'd have to show it if they applied for a job, and they wanted to know what Jesse Jackson did and on and on and on. My patience was all but gone after a day of carting them around and keeping an eye on them. I kept responding with one-word answers, except when I turned and scowled, "Didn't you just ask me that already?" I could only imagine James hollering at the kids in his van to hush their mouths.

By Election Day, some of that excitement had worn off. After registering thirty-eight kids, I could only convince twenty-one of them to come with me and cast their ballots. Once again, we loaded into the van, and I drove them to the senior citizens building over on State Street, where I figured we wouldn't have to fight a big crowd.

I'm sure the building had been quiet before we walked in, but that ended the moment the first kid pushed the door open. All of them were laughing and carrying on like they were in a school cafeteria, their voices echoing off the high ceilings. The older folks serving as election workers weren't too happy about it. They frowned and shushed us like a bunch of librarians. *Calm down, y'all*, I thought. *It's their first time voting. Give them a break.*

If I hadn't been trying to get these kids out of there as fast as possible, I would have been laughing my head off. None of them had ever seen a voting machine before. They'd never taken an official marker and filled out a ballot. A boy named Jaleb kept marking the side of his ballot and then couldn't understand why the voting machine wouldn't accept it.

"I ain't voting," he shouted after the machine spit out his ballot for the second time. "This is too hard."

I could see Senneca tossing down her marker in frustration. "I don't know any of these people!" she whined. "All I know is the president. Who are all these judges and regents?"

I shook my head and laughed. These were tough, hard young people. These were kids who didn't let the threat of drive-bys and gang fights keep them off the streets. And now they were intimidated by a machine and a sheet of paper.

By the time we all finally voted, not one of them would put on their "I voted" sticker. They refused to take a picture with me, shouting that they "ain't no punks." But when we walked out of there, I felt like I'd just won an election myself. These strong, black teenagers had power just by casting their vote.

That night, nobody turned on the TV. We stayed as far away from the news as possible. We kept on doing what we normally did: singing, doing homework, writing poetry, anything to take our minds off the election results pouring in across the country. We knew what the polls said. We knew Obama's chances were good. And yet we were terrified. The kids' words echoed through my head: "They ain't gonna let no black man in there." Even the craziest conspiracy theories seemed plausible that night. *What if somebody fixed the election?* I worried. *What if this whole thing is rigged just to keep a black man out of the White House?*

And then I heard it. Outside, a voice screamed in the silence, piercing through the darkness.

"He won! He won!"

I rushed to my window. There was my neighbor, standing on her porch, screaming as if she'd just won the lottery. "Obama won!"

Could this be real? Could this really happen? One by one, houses in my neighborhood lit up. Neighbors ran out of their houses, all of them screaming. That's when I knew. It was true. America had its first black president.

The kids and I hugged one another and shouted at the top of our lungs as we ran onto my porch to join the celebration. One boy rushed right past us and into the street, pounding on passing cars and even a bus, screaming that Obama had won. My sister, who was at my house, came running downstairs doing her yodel, hollering, "Yiyiyiyiyi!" as Aisha joined in with her. James grabbed the phone and called up every family member he could think of, just to share in the moment with them. And we finally switched on the TV to see the good news for ourselves.

In the middle of the chaos, I turned to see my mom standing in the living room. Her face said it all. "I lived to see this," her bright smile told me. "After all I've lived through, I saw a black man be elected president."

"Let's go downtown!" the kids yelled, tugging at my sleeve. "Let's go watch Obama's speech!" As we spoke, Barack Obama and his family were on their way to Grant Park for his acceptance speech.

I was tempted. Watching him take the stage would be a historic moment unlike anything I'd ever witnessed. But then I remembered the night the Bears won the Super Bowl. It was back in the eighties, and James and I drove downtown to celebrate our hometown team's victory. We returned to our car that night to find it had been trampled by people running out of the bars. The last thing I needed was for a euphoric crowd to destroy our vans. I'd have to be content with watching history happen on my TV.

As President-elect Obama took the stage, I stared at the TV with tears in my eyes, watching him smile and wave to the crowd next to his wife, Michelle, and his little girls, Malia and Sasha. Hope washed over me. The kids felt it too. If America could elect a black president, anything was possible. In a neighborhood that felt hopeless most of the time, this election night was a glimpse of something different. This was proof that these kids had hope, too, beyond the streets and violence. Maybe now they'd believe it.

When I heard a group called Safety Net had rented charter buses to take kids to President Obama's inauguration, I jumped at the opportunity. KOB kids had already played a role in getting Obama elected. Now I wanted them to see the fruits of their labor. I arranged for us to stay in dorms at Howard University while we were in Washington, DC. Not only would these kids get to watch President Obama be sworn in, but they would also step foot on a college campus, some of them for the first time in their lives. I wanted them to see what was possible if they applied themselves. I wanted them to think about their futures and the steps it would take to get there.

The air was a few degrees below freezing when we stepped off the charter bus and trekked toward the National Mall. We were shoulder to shoulder with crowds all headed in the same direction. I wasn't worried about keeping track of everybody in that sea of people. I'd done it so many times at block parties and on bus trips that it was second nature to me now. You couldn't walk without stepping on somebody or somebody stepping on you. But everywhere you looked, people were smiling. I didn't come across a single person who wasn't excited.

We're from Chicago, so we were used to cold weather, but the wind felt especially cold as it cut through our heavy coats.

"Miss Diane, it's freezing!" they complained now and then.

"Y'all be quiet!" one of the older kids would say. "Don't you know how big this is?"

But everybody forgot about the weather as we finally reached the grassy mall and scrunched in next to strangers. Aisha's jaw dropped as she saw the Washington Monument behind us and the US Capitol in front of us. The steps where President Obama would be sworn in were too far away to see, even if you squinted, but giant screens were set up with speakers so you could see and hear everything. I didn't care how far back we were. I just wanted to be there.

As I watched President Obama place his hand on the Bible and take the oath of office, I felt like it wasn't real. Like somebody else was there watching, and I was looking on in the background. I had to pinch myself just to remember it wasn't a dream. The kids didn't laugh or joke even once.

We were all still in disbelief as we toured the Capitol and visited other monuments. We walked the halls of Howard University, where I pointed out pictures of famous alumni like Toni Morrison, Anthony Anderson, and Sean "Puffy" Combs. "That could be you up there one day," I told them. We sat around laughing and joking with Howard students and listened as they told us about their classes, their majors, and their goals. I could see some of the older kids leaning forward with interest.

By the time I loaded them back onto the bus for the twelve-hour drive home, these kids thought they could single-handedly take on the world. They were inspired, hopeful, brimming with confidence.

*I just wish that feeling would last*, I thought. I knew what would happen when they returned home. Their gangs, their poverty, their war-torn streets would be right there waiting for them. It wouldn't be long before hopelessness would creep back in. The high they were riding now would come crashing down.

CHAPTER
TWELVE

# Not on My Block

I felt uneasy every time the warm breeze blew through my window. Summer again. Since I started KOB, I'd known that gang violence heated up with the summer temperatures. I knew to look over my shoulder, to notice every silhouette moving down the alley, to check every car slowly rolling down the road.

But the summer of 2009 was different. New gangs were popping up left and right. Normally, the gangs kept to their own blocks. You knew not to cross into somebody else's territory unless you were looking for trouble. The members of these new gangs, however, lived on the same street. They knew where their rivals played basketball, bought pop, and chilled with their friends. They knew when somebody left their house and when they came home. Anybody who walked out their front door was an easy target. And every day, somebody was into it with somebody else.

So everybody stayed inside as much as they could. Playgrounds were even emptier than usual, and yards were still. Kids called me asking for rides to KOB so they didn't have to risk the walk.

If you asked me, I'd tell you I saw this coming a full two years earlier. I remember rising to my feet and shouting, "It's about time!" when I saw on the news that Robert Taylor, one of Chicago's infamous high-rise housing projects, had been demolished. Families who'd lived there were resettled throughout the city, including in Roseland. If they'd asked me, I'd have told them they better make sure they don't put rival gangs on the same block. City leaders didn't consider that moving new gangs into a community could spark a war.

Sending these families of the projects out into neighborhoods without careful planning was like lighting a powder keg. I should know. Back when I was twenty-seven years old, I spent a summer living in Robert Taylor with the six children I had at that time.

My life was in a full tailspin downward when I ended up in the high-rise. I had just divorced my ex-husband after discovering he was messing around with another girl. Then our house caught fire and burned beyond repair. I had no job, no money, and no choice but to bring my babies with me to Robert Taylor.

All seven of us crammed into a three-bedroom apartment on the fourth floor, next to an elevator that never worked. Everything was beige—the cheap tile, the plaster walls that shed flakes I had to keep my children from putting in their mouths. The whole place was empty, no furniture except a few mattresses on the floor. I couldn't afford anything else. None of the apartments had phones. If you wanted to make a call, you had to take the stairs all the way to the first floor and walk outside to a pay phone. At night, I lay awake listening to my neighbors arguing through the paper-thin walls. Sirens and gunshots woke me on the off chance I fell asleep.

Even though we were surrounded by other families in the same boat, I felt completely isolated—we couldn't go outside for fear of getting caught up in one of the gang fights constantly breaking out. I couldn't even call my family unless I wanted to brave the outdoors. Each day I'd watch my children cooped up in that horrible apartment and feel like I'd failed. Maybe if I'd made better choices, been a better mother, we wouldn't be here.

My sixteen-year-old sister came to stay with me that summer to help me out. She knew it might be dangerous, but even she was caught off guard when she was constantly heckled and catcalled by gang members roaming around the building. Then one night, I heard her screaming in the hallway before she opened the door. I took one look at her, covered in blood, and screamed along with her. It was several minutes before she could find the words to tell me what had happened: a thirteen-year-old boy chased her with a knife trying to stab her until she grabbed the knife and stabbed him in self-defense.

Our nightmare became an all-out hell on earth. My sister was sent to jail, though the judge would later throw out the case since she was attacked. Everybody in the projects turned against us, even though she'd acted in self-defense. If we stayed, we could get hurt, or worse. So in the middle of the night, I sneaked my babies out and moved into my auntie's basement. Even after all the terrifying moments I've experienced since then, I still look back on that time as the scariest summer of my life.

The hopelessness I'd felt living in Robert Taylor had been overwhelming. I knew what the new families in our neighborhood were going through. But I also knew that plopping them down in a community with no support and no forethought was going to be trouble. Especially when some of the boys in KOB were into it with the new gangs that had moved onto the block.

We were out on the vacant lot across the street every day with our rolling basketball hoop. All day long, kids would play three-on-three while everybody else watched from the benches James had built. I'd never given a thought to being on the lot, out in the open, with no fences or structures to shield us. I wasn't blind—I knew some of the boys were in gangs—but as far as I was concerned, they didn't bring that mess with them when they were at KOB. It wasn't long, though, before I saw a car I didn't recognize roll by slowly. Boys glared at us as they flashed gang signs out the window.

My heart pounded as I kept my eyes on that car, waiting for a gun barrel to appear. It turned the corner and disappeared.

"Those boys don't like us," DaJuan told me, shaking his head. "They into it with Levi's crew."

I turned my head and glanced at Levi, wearing his hoodie and baggy jeans even though that afternoon's temperatures easily topped eighty degrees. This was the same boy who had bragged to me on my porch years earlier about how he "got that meat." I had hoped all my speeches about turning your life around and solving your problems without guns would have rubbed off by now.

I felt more and more exposed each time we rolled the basketball hoop onto the lot. I never asked the kids to stay inside. I wasn't going to let a few gangbangers intimidate us. But I kept an eye toward Michigan Avenue just in case.

We were in the middle of a basketball game one day when one of the boys tapped me on my shoulder. "Miss Diane, these boys are coming down the alley," he said quietly, his voice nervous.

I kept calm even as I felt my stomach flip-flop. "Okay, let me go look."

The handful of boys creeping up the alley weren't hidden. I knew who they were, even in their hoodies. I knew they were from the gang that had battled with Levi's gang all summer.

I didn't have time to turn or warn anybody else. Before I could open my mouth, I saw one of the boys reach into his pocket. I saw a flash of metal, a hard stare on the boy's face. And then, bullets. My ears rang as shots fired and bullets popped from the biggest handgun I'd ever seen.

"Everybody, get down!" I shouted as the other boys grabbed their guns, spraying bullets around the court. The kids screamed, scrambling over cars and across the street to get inside my house.

Levi, meanwhile, pulled out two guns from his pockets and charged toward the boys in the alley, shooting with every step he took. I screamed at him to put the guns down, but it was no use. My voice was lost in the crash of gunfire.

Thank the Lord, not one of those boys knew what they were doing with a gun. They couldn't hit the broad side of a brick wall. I looked around wildly for anybody lying on the ground, praying nobody got shot. Bullets rained down around us, but my mind was fixed on protecting the kids.

*Lord, just keep these kids safe*, I prayed over and over. *If even one of them got hurt, I could never forgive myself.*

I called the police and hoped that would be the end of it. But it wasn't. This wasn't just one gang we were dealing with here. We were talking about rival gangs from all over the city, now living in our neighborhood.

When the kids showed up for programming, I wanted to tell them we were staying indoors. *Maybe we shouldn't be out there*, I thought. *Maybe it's not worth the risk.*

But the kids weren't having it. "Miss Diane, we out here," they'd say. "This is our lot."

I took in the line of defiant faces—not just the boys, but also Aisha, Senneca, and Brittany. Every last one of them was in agreement.

Now, my faith was strong. I knew God would protect us. But the way I see it, you don't just walk into a lion's den. Even Daniel didn't walk into the den himself. He had to be thrown in, and even then I imagine he was probably kicking and screaming. But these kids were determined. This was their home. Shootings happened. Like it or not, they were used to it. They couldn't let it keep them down.

And so we kept going. We couldn't let the gangs intimidate us. If we stayed inside, that meant they won. They would have accomplished exactly what they wanted. Every single day, no matter who shot whom the night before, we dragged that old rolling basketball hoop across the street again. "Miss Diane, we out here," they'd say again, their eyes lit with that same fire. "We ain't going anywhere."

Our defiance wasn't enough to stop the violence. At first, I'd hear about somebody's cousin or friend getting shot a few blocks over. Then one night, a boy who went by the name Smoke came running down the sidewalk and up my steps. I could hear him panting to catch his breath as he banged on my front door. It was about nine o'clock and not quite dark yet when I brought him inside. I knew without asking that something terrible had happened.

"Jason's been shot," he managed to get out between gasps for air.

I closed my eyes. *Not Jason. Lord have mercy.* Jason had been in and out of hospitals since the day I'd met him. The poor boy was born with a heart condition, and I always brought a vanload of kids to visit him every time he had an operation. He was a sweet boy, but I knew he was in a clique over in his neighborhood. Everybody told him to stay off 119th Street. That was rival gang territory. That street was trouble for anybody in Jason's clique. But every time I turned around, he was over there anyway. The kids whispered that he had his eye on a girl over there. And now he'd been shot.

"Where is he?" I demanded.

"He's on his way to Christ," Smoke said, meaning Advocate Christ Medical Center in Oak Lawn.

"Where was he shot at? Is he okay?"

"We don't know."

I nodded. I knew what I had to do next. I had to call Jason's mother.

Jason, it turned out, would be fine. He had been shot in the groin and made a full recovery. But he wasn't the last KOB boy who was shot that summer. Next came Rayshawn. Then TO caught a bullet. And Traveon. These weren't the only kids in Roseland who got shot that summer. These were just the ones I knew personally. All of them survived, thank God. But every time I learned another kid I loved had been shot, the more I felt like a failure. I'd spent the last six years trying to get these boys out of gangs, show them another way, keep them safe. With these battles raging in my neighborhood, I felt like I didn't stand a chance.

I couldn't sit back and let it happen anymore. There had to be something I could do. I had to take a stand and find a way to keep these kids safe.

My first idea was to go straight to the gang leaders and talk to them myself. I have no idea what I thought I'd say or how that could possibly work. But I was determined. When I approached DaJuan with the idea, though, he shook his head.

"Miss Diane, they ain't gonna listen," he said. "You can't talk to them."

He eventually let me talk to one of his friends who was in with a gang leader. When that boy told me the same thing DaJuan had, I knew I needed a different approach. Much as I didn't want to, I got the police involved. I made another trip to my district and sat down with Commander Ball. I told him about the shooting on the lot, about all the boys who'd had guns pointed at them this summer. From then on, a police car sat on my block for a few hours each night. And it helped. Nobody shot at anybody on my block as long as the police were there. But they couldn't sit there twenty-four hours a day. The police couldn't clean up our block for us. We'd have to do it ourselves.

Here in Roseland, every block is somebody's territory. Everybody knows who's in charge when you cross from one street to the next. This little stretch of Michigan Avenue wasn't going to be like that, I decided. This block belonged to KOB.

"These gangs don't run this block," I vented to James one night. "This is our block. These folks are gonna respect that this is KOB territory. I ain't gonna have this violence anymore. Not on my block."

I wasn't the only one raising up the battle cry. DaJuan, Richard, Aisha, and several of the older kids were fed up with the gangs creeping up on our territory. For the first time, they had opinions when I mentioned block parties and rallies, telling me where we should go and who we should and shouldn't follow.

The boys who loved rapping wrote their own positive lyrics, urging kids to stop throwing their lives away and to stay off the streets. Other organizations took notice and invited them to perform at events. Each time they did, we'd all roll in wearing our airbrushed KOB shirts so everybody knew who we were.

I'd tried for years to get the kids to speak to reporters or take the microphone at rallies. Everybody would much rather hear from them than from me. Now they were speaking up. I didn't even have to ask—they'd come to me asking if they could say something.

Our street cred went up several notches more when we tricked out one of our vans. A police officer had donated a van years before—with its plush interior, it looked like something pimps would drive around. With the help of a grant, we had a printing company create giant pictures of a few KOB boys and plaster them on the sides of the van. After a few weeks of riding around like that, every kid in the neighborhood recognized us when we rolled into a block party. "That's KOB!" they'd whisper excitedly. Those boys walked around with their chests all puffed out. That hood fame went straight to their heads.

It wasn't about getting famous or making sure people knew our names. It was about defending our home—our Roseland. Every event, every outing, every trip raised our profile. People understood who we were and what we were doing. They knew we weren't going anywhere. They knew we wouldn't turn a kid away, no matter what gang he belonged to or who his daddy was.

So, slowly, they started to respect us. Neighbors showed up with a bag of shoes asking if I thought any of the KOB kids might like them. Caterers called me offering trays of food to help support the Thanksgiving feast we hosted each year. Meanwhile, new kids walked through my door as my regulars were telling all their friends about the bus trip we had just taken to Birmingham, Alabama, or the presents they got at the Christmas party we'd held the night before.

We'd been on the block for years, but this was the first time I truly felt KOB had come into its own. We knew who we were and what we did. Now everybody else did too.

When that summer wound to a close, I was ready to celebrate. The gangs wanted us to leave, but we didn't. They wanted us to hide in fear, but we kept showing up anyway. No matter what they did, we were out there. That was worth remembering in some kind of special way.

When I told the kids my idea, they asked if I'd lost my mind. I'd seen all kinds of videos blowing up on YouTube of huge groups dancing to Michael Jackson's "Thriller." I thought the kids would be excited about the possibility of KOB being the next viral sensation. They didn't quite see it that way.

"We ain't no punks!" they shouted.

But somehow, when I walked out to the lot one late-August day, fifty-five kids followed me. They may have rolled their eyes and hid their faces behind their hoodies so their friends wouldn't see them if they drove by. But when I hit Play, they laughed their heads off as they slid their feet and popped their hips to the beat. Tears streamed down my cheeks as I tried not to pee my pants from laughing so hard.

As I looked around the lot, taking in the dozens of embarrassed teenagers in front of me, I realized I couldn't remember the last time somebody slow-rolled by the lot, throwing up a gang sign. All these months, we kept going even as we looked over our shoulders, never knowing who might come down the alley. By God's grace, we were brave enough to keep going. And now, somehow, we had won. The neighborhood had conceded—this block belonged to KOB. This was our territory. And nobody would scare us off. Not now. Not ever.

## CHAPTER THIRTEEN

# Turn Around

"Miss D! You gotta see this!" The voice echoed from the little music studio down the hall. I told the kids sitting at the computers that I'd be back to help them with their homework, and then I started searching for whoever was calling me, ducking between chairs and dodging dancing girls as I headed to the back room.

There were Zeek and Jordan, grinning like little kids and bobbing their heads to music that played on their headphones. Zeek slipped off his headphones and grinned at me.

"We recorded a new song, Miss D!" He motioned for me to come inside—not that I really fit. The room was already crammed with amps, speakers, and a table set up with a mixing board and computer. There was just enough room for two people to sit in chairs and record inside the walls lined with soundproofing foam.

I squeezed behind the boys' chairs and pulled the headphones over my ears. Jordan turned toward me excitedly. "You ready?" he asked before he hit Play.

"We callin' this 'The Movement,'" Zeek said.

A thumping beat pulsed through the headphones. I could hear Zeek's and Jordan's voices rapping along with one of their friends.

> Let's do it, let's do it
> KOB is the movement
> If you wanna be successful, you gotta prove it
> Man, they think we're stupid, they don't think we can
>     do it,
> So do it, and prove it
> Show 'em there's nothing to it

"Oooh, I like that," I told them, bobbing my head to the slick track backing up their voices. "Y'all sound real good."

I tried not to let them see the tears of pride at the corners of my eyes. I still could hardly believe that these two boys were KOB leaders these days, that they were out rapping positive messages and taking young boys under their wings. I knew they had it in them, I thought. But back when Zeek first walked through my door in 2009, it sure seemed like a long shot.

Zeek walked in behind his cousin Delores, his giant lips sticking out in a pout so far I could see it from across the room. I guessed he was about eighteen years old, with light skin, his hair cut in a low fade. Everything he was wearing, from his low-riding blue jeans to his cute little T-shirt, was chosen carefully. This boy wanted to create a certain image for himself, and from the way he rolled his eyes as Delores pulled him toward me, that image was too cool for KOB.

"I told Zeek about you, Miss Diane," Delores said after she'd introduced us. "I told him you be helping us, and he need to come talk to you."

"Oh really?" I asked casually. He didn't seem too interested in what an old lady had to say.

"He ain't in a gang or nothing," Delores said after Zeek sauntered away and slouched down in a computer chair. "But he's got an attitude problem. I told him you can help us through all that kind of stuff."

I fixed my eyes on her cousin. The boy's lips were now twisted into a smirk, as if everybody in the room was beneath him. "Does he want help?" Lord knows you can't help somebody with an attitude problem if they don't think they need it.

Delores shrugged. "I don't know. But if he don't get it, his mama gonna end up kicking him out."

I walked into the dining room. *Lord, You gotta work on this boy's heart*, I prayed. *I can't help him if he ain't ready.*

Zeek didn't say much as I checked on how kids were doing with their homework and asked them about their day. I loved hearing their stories and listening to them crack jokes. I had everybody right where I wanted them. All of us squeezed into the room like sardines in a can, laughing and going back and forth. All of us except Zeek. By now he was slouched down so far in his chair he was practically lying on the seat, that smirk still on his face. Everything about his attitude screamed, "I'm too good for y'all. Y'all are punks."

I was patient, at first. I asked him questions, tried to make him feel included. He didn't answer a single one with more than a shrug or a grunt. *Maybe he's nervous*, I thought. *Maybe he's just worried about fitting in*. But the more he smirked, the more irritated I became.

I'd worked with kids long enough by then to know that attitudes are contagious. If I let one boy get away with acting like he's something else, I'd have a whole room full of kids thinking the sun shines out of their backsides. The last thing I needed was for kids to clap back at me like, "Well, you let Zeek do it!"

So after one smirk too many, I turned to face him.

"Okay, what's your problem?" I said bluntly.

Zeek started, like he hadn't expected me to call him out. "I ain't got no problem," he muttered.

"Oh, yes you do." This boy wasn't getting me off his back that easily. "But I just want to know what it is so I can help you with it."

"You can't help me." Zeek's voice was cold, defiant.

I shook my head and sighed. "Oh, you think that already, huh?"

There it was again. That smirk. "You can't make me do nothing."

I bit my lip to keep words from flying out that I'd have to repent of later. If there was one thing that infuriated me, it was some punk kid walking into my house acting like he was in charge.

"Well, you in my house, dude." I locked eyes with him, my face dead serious. "Why are you here again?"

Now Zeek sat up straight. I could tell I'd gotten to him. "I don't have to be here," he shot back.

"Well, get to steppin'," I said, motioning toward the door.

Zeek popped out of his chair in a huff, muttering curse words as he stomped through the living room and slammed the front door. Delores looked at me apologetically before she chased after him, begging him to come back inside.

A few minutes later, there he was again, flopping down in his chair like nothing happened.

"Oh no," I hollered, wagging my finger at him. "You ain't coming back until you apologize."

Zeek's face contorted with confusion. NBA players acting like they didn't just commit a foul had nothing on this boy. "I didn't do nothing!"

"You did something." I kept my voice calm but firm. "You don't come in here with that attitude. If something's bothering you, let's talk about it. But you ain't sitting in here acting like you're too good to be here."

I wasn't sure if I'd ever see Zeek again after he walked down the front steps with Delores and headed home. He sure didn't act like he was interested in anything we did. My skin crawled every time I thought of that smirk.

But the next day, there he was, attitude and all. Day after day, he kept showing up. And every day, he had another excuse for why he slouched in his chair, refusing to talk. Sometimes it was because his mama yelled at him. Sometimes it was because he missed his dad, who he hadn't seen since he was a kid. Other times it was because he'd gotten into it with somebody on the bus earlier that day.

I wasn't having those excuses. It's not that I'm cold and insensitive. His issues weighed heavily on his shoulders. This boy wasn't the only one. Literally every kid at KOB had problems. I'd spent the last six years listening to kids tell me about their mom yelling at them or their auntie in the hospital or a friend who'd passed. But Zeek couldn't see that. Whatever issue he had that day was worse than anybody else's, no matter what it was. If he didn't want to talk about it and deal with the problem, I wasn't interested in hearing about it. Most of the time, his excuse led to an argument that got him kicked out.

"What's that got to do with the price of beans?" I'd say when he offered me another lame excuse for why he was treating me like dirt.

Zeek looked at me like I'd lost my mind. "Huh? What's that mean?"

"That's old school," I said. "It means, what's that got to do with me?" Before he could smirk at me, I kept going. "Whatever happened, you can tell everybody about it. This is a safe place. But then release it. Let it go. Don't bring it here."

He stared at the ground, refusing to speak. *I'm gonna get him*, I thought, determined. *One of these days, I'm gonna get him*. This kid wanted help. Why else would he show up day after day, even when I kicked him out? Deep down, he knew he needed something that he couldn't get on his own. Every day when he walked through my front door, I was hopeful. *Maybe this is the day*, I thought. *Maybe today he's ready*.

Sure enough, something was different one day. Zeek slouched down in his chair and stuck out his lip like usual. But something in his eyes told me this wasn't about some argument on the bus or his mama telling him to take out the trash. Something deeper was going on here.

"Zeek, what's going on?" I didn't expect him to say much. He never had before. But this time, he looked up at me with his big eyes and sighed.

"My mom said I gotta get a job," he said quietly. "She said I gotta get on my feet and help out. Or else I gotta find my own place." He stopped himself from saying more, as if he might start crying.

I sat down in the chair next to him, laying my hand gently on his shoulder. "Zeek, your mom is right. You a grown man now. If your mama needs help, you gotta get a job or do something."

You could have knocked me over with a feather when the next thing I knew, Zeek scrunched up his face and broke down in tears. Every trace of swag was gone. The boy held his face in his hands and leaned into his knees. I forgot about how much he irritated me, or how he'd disrespected me in my house. None of that mattered anymore. My mother instincts took over as I scooped him up and held him.

"I do want to help my mom," he sobbed, his tears flowing freely now. "I don't want to sell drugs. I want a real job."

I kept on rubbing his back, trying to comfort him. "Well, have you tried getting one?"

Zeek sighed. "I've tried, Miss D." He had called me Miss D since the first day he'd walked into my house. "It ain't that easy. While I was in school, I tried. I worked a couple of jobs. They didn't work out."

I pushed him back for a moment so I could look him in the eye. "Zeek, do you think your attitude is the problem?"

I waited for him to pull away in anger, to stand up and march out of the house. But instead, ever so slightly, he nodded. "It could be, Miss D."

We didn't speak. I waited for him to keep going. Zeek was opening up for the first time, and I didn't want to say or do anything to make him clam back up. Finally, he spoke again. "I'm angry. I'm angry because my dad was not in my life."

His words tugged at my heart in a way he couldn't have understood. Instantly, I was a little girl again in my mind, watching my friends with their daddies and wishing I had one, too, asking my mama why my daddy didn't come take me fishing or to the movies.

"Zeek," I said slowly, "I know exactly how you feel."

Zeek looked up, tears still running down his face.

"I hadn't seen my father since I was five years old," I told him as other kids gathered around to listen. "He came to pick me up one day. He took me to his mom's house, and I stayed with them for five days. It might have been a little longer. I remember riding around in a little white convertible with the top down. I loved feeling the wind in my hair and laughing with him next to me. He brought me home to my mama. And then I didn't see him again."

Zeek nodded. I noticed a few other kids with eyes shining from tears. It was a story too familiar in our community, a story of growing up without a father.

"When I was seven years old, my mama told me why I hadn't seen my daddy. She told me he was in an explosion at his job. His brother was killed, and my daddy had burns over 90 percent of his body." I saw a few surprised faces in the room. That's not where they thought my story was going.

"I had this fantasy that when my daddy got better, he'd come get me and we'd be a family. But he didn't. So I looked for him. All those years, I dreamed that when I found him, he would wrap me up in his arms and hug me and tell me how glad he was to see me."

I swallowed before I kept going. No matter how many years had gone by, this story didn't get any easier.

"I finally found him when I was twenty-eight years old. But he wasn't glad to see me. He said, 'I already have my family. I don't want you here.'"

I heard an audible gasp in the room as I finished. Everybody scooted closer to one another. One by one, they shared their stories. Stories of fathers they'd never met. Stories of fathers they wished they'd never met. I'd held it together the whole time I'd told them about my father, but one story from the kids and I was done. It seemed like everybody in the room was sobbing, and I was crying right along with them.

Finally, I stopped them. *What can I do, God?* I prayed. *I can help a kid get back in school or fight for them to get out of a gang. I can help a homeless kid find a place to stay until their parents take them back in. But a hurt like this? I know that hurt. I don't want nobody else to feel it. Ain't nobody can help them but You.*

"Everybody grab hands," I said. "We gonna pray."

Somebody switched on a Yolanda Adams gospel album as I called out to the Lord there in my living room. Her soaring voice filled the air as I asked God to heal each and every one of these kids, to fill the hole left behind by their fathers, to replace their anger with peace. Everybody, from young teenage girls to hardened gang members, sniffled and wiped their eyes. The Holy Ghost was there in that room. You could feel it. You could sense it in the way nobody wanted to move, even after I finished praying. Nobody wanted to play basketball or pick up trash on the block. Nobody wanted to rap or dance. We stayed there in the living room, talking and praying, long after the sun set.

Zeek's attitude completely disappeared after that day. The sweet, caring boy hiding inside of him was now visible for all to see. This boy was like my right-hand man, taking charge and making sure the other kids went along with whatever we were doing that day. His smirk was replaced with a grin. Instead of sitting back and refusing to speak, Zeek was in the middle of everything. My heart just about exploded with pride every time I saw the way the other kids looked at him, like he was the kind of person they wanted to be one day. *I knew it*, I'd think, watching him from across the room. *I knew I'd get him.*

Jordan and Zeek watched me closely as I listened to their song. They weren't disappointed—I oohed and aahed over the lyrics and swayed along to the music.

> You better wise up before your time up
> And if you need a mentor,
> I'm right here
> For real

I nudged Jordan playfully on the shoulder. "Jordan the mentor," I joked. "You sure you wanna put that in your song? You don't want the whole neighborhood banging on your door."

Jordan laughed. "I'm serious, Miss D! I'll mentor anybody. I really mean that."

I knew he meant it. It seemed like every night, Jordan was picking up boys from his street after school and taking them to basketball games or out for pizza at Pizza Hut. He blushed red as a firecracker under his coffee-colored skin when he brought three of the boys he was mentoring to meet me. Those boys looked at him like he was Michael Jordan. He was a celebrity in their eyes, a cool older boy who was going places, and here he was taking an afternoon to spend time with them.

Back in 2009, most boys would have been scared to hang out with Jordan alone. He was in his early twenties when he first showed up on the lot with TO to play basketball. The other kids froze as he hollered, "Can I play?"

"That's Jordan," I heard somebody whisper.

Jordan's family had lived in Roseland as long as anybody could remember. Everybody knew who he was. He was one of the few boys in the neighborhood who drove a car, and everybody said he always kept two guns in the trunk. Everybody kept their eyes on that car and held their breath anytime he came near it.

I'd never had a conversation with Jordan, mostly because he never came inside my house. Once basketball was over for the day, he'd wave to me and yell, "Hey, Miss D!" before climbing in his car and disappearing down the street.

So when I heard a knock on my door one September night, Jordan was the last person I expected to see when I opened it.

"Can I talk to you, Miss D?" he asked quietly.

I studied his face, wondering what was going on behind those dark eyes of his. "Of course," I said, opening the door wider. "Come on in."

Jordan sighed as he sat down on a folding chair and set his backpack on the floor. He leaned into his knees, still wearing his jacket, as he hung his head and stared at the ground.

"Miss D, this dude just beat up my sister." He paused for a moment, pressing his lips together tightly, fury written all over his face. "I was going to shoot him. But something told me to come here first."

My mind raced. This boy had never stepped foot in my house or said anything to me beyond a greeting. I didn't know he thought enough of me to ask me for advice, let alone that he would be asking about shooting somebody. *Don't yell*, I thought. *Keep your cool. Talk some sense into him.*

"Jordan," I said slowly, "you a leader. But you a negative leader."

Jordan frowned. "What do you mean?"

"These boys in the neighborhood look up to you. But they're scared of you. They think what you're doing is exciting. They think you don't take no mess. But just think about what would happen if you were a positive leader. What if you were leading boys to do the right thing? What kind of impact could you have?"

Jordan was silent for a moment. "I don't want to be a negative leader," he said. "I don't want everybody to be scared of me. But this place ain't safe. I can't trust nobody. Now this dude beats up my sister. And I'm supposed to let him just get away with it?"

I sat down next to him and placed my hand on his knee. "You have a right to feel like that. You're right. This place ain't safe. But you could change that."

He shook his head. "How am I supposed to do that?"

"You can start with your situation. How you handle it. If you shoot this boy, that ain't gonna make the neighborhood safer. It sure ain't gonna make your family safer." I looked into his eyes, so dark I could see my reflection in them. "I can't make the decision for you. You have to do it."

Jordan must have sat in my living room for two and a half hours before he finally picked up his backpack. "I want to get out of these streets, Miss D," he said as he stood. "I really do want to change."

I exhaled as he walked out the front door, trying to slow my pounding heart. *God, I don't know which way this boy is gonna go*, I prayed. *I said everything I could. Please let him make the right choice.*

I barely slept that night. When I finally drifted off, I heard gunshots in my dreams. I startled awake, sure that I heard my phone ring, sure that somebody would be on the other line telling me Jordan was locked up for murder.

But when kids arrived for programming the next day, there was Jordan, smiling. "Hey, Miss D!" he called like nothing had happened. He nodded slightly as I locked eyes with him. He didn't say anything else, but I knew he'd done the right thing.

I wouldn't learn the full story until months later, when *Essence* magazine called me up asking for an interview. They were looking for a kid to include in their story. Jordan was the one to pop into my head. By then, he was known throughout the streets as Jordan the Mentor. He'd taken my words to heart. Nobody could call him a negative leader now. He was on a mission to lead young boys down the right path. So I gave the *Essence* writer his phone number.

When I read the article, I nearly dropped the magazine. There in black-and-white print was a quote from Jordan saying that night in my house, he had the gun in his backpack. He had every intention of leaving my house and walking straight to that boy's house to shoot him. I'll never know what made him come to my house. I'll never know what made him turn around and go home.

I look at boys like Jordan and Zeek, boys who walked into my house one way and walked out completely different. I look at the conversations we had, the advice I gave them, the prayers I prayed when they left. Truth is, nothing I said was particularly special or unusual. And yet God used it. God used me. These boys turned their lives around, and I got to play a role in their story. Those are the moments that light my heart on fire, the moments that get me out of bed in the morning and push me to keep going.

But not every story has a happy ending. I'd find that out soon enough.

## CHAPTER FOURTEEN

# No Peace

I tried to hide my grin as I scanned my living room for TO. He didn't smile much. He kept his face fixed in a scowl, only breaking from his tough-guy persona when he hit a tough shot on the basketball court. But today would be different. Today, I'd see his face light up with pure joy.

I found him standing over the kids doing homework. TO wasn't much interested in his own schoolwork, but he was all too happy to help the other kids—the kids he liked, anyway. Nobody really asked for his help, but they got it whether they wanted it or not.

"No, dude, you sound stupid if you spell the word like that!" he'd holler when somebody asked for help with spelling. Not exactly the way I would approach helping a kid with their homework.

"TO!" I shouted to get his attention. He jerked his head up, startled.

"I didn't curse, Miss Diane!" he protested. "Don't get me with your pen!"

I burst out laughing. "No, no, no. I got something to tell you."

Now I had his attention.

"We starting an after-school basketball program. This group called After School Cares is giving us money to run it. And they said I can hire an assistant." I kept grinning. "I'm thinking that assistant should be you."

TO looked like a kid who'd just unwrapped the biggest gift on Christmas morning. His smile was so wide I could see just about every tooth in his mouth. "You get paid for that?" he asked in disbelief.

I nodded. "Yep. As long as you show up and do what I tell you. Maybe you can save up for a new pair of Jordans."

"Aw, man, I can't wait to whip y'all into shape!" TO yelled. I wondered if he might bounce up and down with excitement. This boy loved nothing more than basketball. He would go anywhere and do anything if it meant he got to dribble and shoot. And now I was telling him he would get paid for it.

I watched TO brag to the other boys about his new job. *He's gonna make it*, I thought. *He's gonna be alright*.

Each day, TO was already waiting on his front porch when I picked him up and drove him to the basketball program. He strode onto the court in shorts and a T-shirt, a whistle around his neck—at least on the days when we could find one.

I told him his job was to make sure the program ran smoothly, and he took that assignment to heart. For those hours on the court, he was a man with a purpose. He met with the coaches to let them know if we were running layup drills or if a speaker was stopping by that day. He stocked coolers full of juices and

Gatorades and set up tables with bags of chips, hot dogs, and sandwiches when the local Catholic Charities provided them. And since we were required to document what we did and report it to After School Cares, TO took detailed notes at every single practice.

When he was on the court, he lost every trace of the puffed-up boy I had first met on the lot. He wasn't demanding or controlling or trying to prove himself. Instead, he was out there laughing and telling jokes with the other kids like he was one of them. Like they were all in it together, like a team.

Afterward, we'd hop back in my car for the ride home. Sometimes he was quiet. Other times he'd vent about whatever was bothering him that day—usually something about his mom. He'd lean the passenger seat back and complain that she didn't want him hanging out after nine o'clock at night or wearing certain colors or walking in certain neighborhoods.

*Well, can you blame her?* I wanted to shoot back. TO was still in a gang. He didn't talk about it, but I heard the other kids whisper when he wasn't around. *All your mama wants is for you to stay alive!* I thought. *One day you'll understand.* But I kept my mouth shut. After barely saying a word to me all this time, TO was finally opening up. The last thing I wanted was for him to build his walls back up right as they were coming down. So I'd just say, "Well, that's your mom."

The thing was, TO had potential. Not just on the basketball court, though he certainly had that going on. He was the star of his high school team, despite his penchant for fouling. The KOB kids and I used to cheer on the sidelines as he played point guard, spinning and throwing up shots that we thought were impossible, only for the ball to fall through the hoop. He was quick and calculating, dribbling and running around his opponents before they ever saw him coming. He had his sights set on playing for the Chicago Bulls one day, and I honestly believed he could do it. In our neighborhood, most kids don't dream of being CEOs, lawyers, or doctors. The way they see it, they have two options for getting out of the streets—becoming a rapper or an NBA player. I tried telling them that their chances of making it were slim to nil, that they needed a backup plan. They needed a more realistic option. But TO would just smile at me with that cocky grin of his. "I'm gonna make it, Miss Diane."

Off the court, TO was a leader. Kids wanted to follow him, even if they were scared. I had this feeling that if I could help TO direct his potential in the right way, he would take off and bring the other kids with him. If he changed his attitude, other kids would change, too, just because they wanted to be like him. Even after seven years, I was still figuring it out as I went along, praying God would show me what each kid needed and how to interact with them most effectively. When it came to TO, I knew his language was basketball. I knew this after-school program was my best chance of getting through to him.

So every day, when he climbed into my car venting about his mama running out of food or not getting him the right supplies for a school project, I listened. I didn't judge. I didn't fuss at him, much as I might have wanted to. I didn't give up on him even after he and his rival about started a gun battle on the Curtis Elementary School basketball court. He didn't start it, after all. And he kept coming back, even when he threatened to walk away and never return.

*If I can just get this boy to trust me, I know I can get through to him*, I thought.

Then one day, my phone rang. “Miss Diane, what are you doing?” I heard TO say on the other end. Before I could answer, he announced, “I’m on my way over. I’ll be there soon.”

I stared at the phone after he hung up, wondering what in the world had just happened. TO had never, not even once, called to let me know he was coming. Matter of fact, I was pretty sure that if our basketball hoop ever broke and I didn’t buy a new one, he’d stop showing up. But something had changed. *He cares*, I thought. *And he believes that I care too.*

After that phone call, TO was different. Instead of getting pricked with my pen for cursing, TO was now my enforcer, calling out anybody who got an attitude with me and warning them, “Don’t you talk to Miss Diane like that.” Every day, he showed up ready to roll, asking me, “What are we doing today? What can I do to help?” It was like he’d named himself my permanent KOB assistant, not just at the basketball program. He loved being in charge. He thrived off of it. Whether it was picking up garbage off the block or handing out the breakfasts we got from Catholic Charities, I tried to find odd jobs for him, anything to show him that he was needed. That he could be a leader without being in a gang.

Every time I asked him for help, TO responded like a dog who sees his leash and knows he’s going for a walk. Even when the job in front of him was in direct conflict with gang life. Like the time nobody had seen Jamal for a day and a half—a lifetime for him, considering he hated to be out of my sight.

“Anybody know where Jamal is?” I asked when he didn’t show up for the second day in a row. TO shuffled his feet and looked around nervously. He and Jamal didn’t speak much. When they weren’t in my house, they roamed the streets in rival gangs. They never talked to me about it, but I’m not stupid. I heard the kids talk when they thought I wasn't around. I knew their gangs were into it with one another. I could sense the tension radiating from TO's body as I leaned over Jamal or anybody else in a rival gang to help them with their homework. His eyes never left us, but he never moved. He never got involved. He kept his cool. My job was to keep it that way, to make sure they stayed calm—and that they weren't plotting to shoot at one another as soon as they left.

I couldn't let myself wonder if TO had a gun tucked into his hoodie or if Jamal was packing heat. I didn't spend every day on my soapbox preaching for them to get rid of their weapons and learn to get along. My strategy was to point them toward the future, to show them what was possible and what they were risking with every gang battle. As long as they were in my house, I kept them so busy they didn't have time to get into it.

TO was the last person I expected to be concerned about finding Jamal. But that day he spoke up. "You want me to look for him?"

"No, no," I stammered, caught off guard. "You ain't gotta do that. You got things to do."

"Miss Diane, that other stuff isn't important," he said seriously. "We gotta see if he's okay."

Before I could protest, he took off with two of his boys to hit the street. "You tell Jamal that if he ain't in my house by nine o'clock, I'm calling the police!" I called out after them.

I wasn't under any illusions about TO's motive. That boy wasn't worried about Jamal. He just wanted to be in charge. He liked the idea of leading a search and coming back like a hero with Jamal under his arm. But it was also a step in the right direction. The TO that first walked onto the lot wouldn't have concerned himself with going out looking for anybody from a rival gang. I'm not even sure if he would have searched for somebody from his own gang. The old TO was only worried about himself.

TO didn't end up finding him. Jamal showed up on my doorstep not one minute past nine—just in time to avoid a call to the police. He'd been hiding out at his cousin's house four blocks from home after he and his mom had a fight. But when we saw Jamal's face, TO grinned just as widely as anybody else. *He's coming around*, I thought. *He's really coming around.*

I pulled the burgundy curtains back from my window and scanned the sidewalk one more time. A few last-minute stragglers were climbing up the front steps, a few faces I recognized. But no TO.

I hadn't seen him all week. Usually if he couldn't make it to programming, he'd call to let me know. Not this week. It was like he'd just disappeared.

"Anybody know where TO is?" I finally asked a few boys I knew hung with him. They exchanged glances before somebody spoke up.

"Miss Diane, he hangin' with his cousin," one boy said. "He just came into town, and TO's rolling with him."

A knot formed in the pit of my stomach. On its face, the explanation made sense. TO was spending time with family. What was wrong with that? But something wasn't right. I could just feel it. Days came and went. Still no sign of TO. *I just need to know he's okay*, I thought. *If I could just see him, I'd feel better.*

When that knot in my stomach wouldn't go away, I sent out a few boys to look for him. I thought if TO knew I was worried, he'd come by at least for a little bit. Just long enough to show me he was doing fine. But instead, the boys came back with a message. "He said he'll be here tomorrow, Miss Diane," they said.

I knew right away that was a lie. TO was trying to keep me off his back.

"Have y'all seen TO at school lately?" I asked around. "He seem okay?"

Craig looked up at me, frowning. "He ain't been coming, Miss Diane," he said quietly.

For a moment I thought I might be sick. TO and I had worked so hard to get his grades up. I'd spent more afternoons than I could count meeting with his high school dean, begging him to let TO retake a test or to help him find a tutor. He'd gone from failing his classes to pulling solid grades. And now he was skipping school. *Something's changed*, I thought. *I just don't know what.*

"Miss Diane, I heard he been smokin' weed with his cousin," Jamal said.

"I heard he been out robbing people," Craig added. "He out running with his gang."

I closed my eyes and sank into my chair. All I could think was, why? Why would this boy who showed so much promise throw it all away? Didn't he see his own potential? Didn't he know these streets would destroy everything he'd worked for?

TO was on my mind constantly. I lay awake at night, staring at the ceiling and praying God would protect him, that He would bring TO back to KOB. I fretted to James and Aisha so much they probably got sick of me.

"You can't help everybody, Diane," James said, rubbing my shoulders. "Not if they don't want to be helped."

I'd thought about TO so much that when I saw him walking down the alley by my house, I wondered if it was just my imagination.

"TO!" I called when I realized he was real.

"Oh, hey, Miss Diane!" he said with the distinct tone of somebody who didn't feel like talking.

"Where you been at?" I asked. "You coming tonight?"

"I been busy," he said, avoiding eye contact with me. His face was different. He was still as good-looking as ever, with his light skin and dreads, still wearing his Bulls jersey and old-school Jordans. But the smile I'd come to know, the light he'd had in his eyes, were gone. That old, hard look was back, the look he'd had when I first met him.

"Really?" I asked, raising my eyebrows. I wasn't having this. "What are you doing, TO? Why haven't you been to program?"

He sighed, clearly frustrated. "Miss Diane, I just been busy. I'll be over there next week."

I pursed my lips. He wasn't going to listen to a word I said. Not much of a point in saying more. "Well, okay. I'll see you then."

I didn't know then that he was on his way to get a gun. I didn't know somebody had threatened him.

TO didn't come the next week. Or the week after that. He never walked through my front door again. He never dribbled the basketball on the lot or corrected anybody's spelling. He never called me to say he was on his way over.

I gave up sending boys to look for him. By now, everybody was talking about him. They told me he was out threatening boys from rival gangs and walking into territory where he shouldn't go. Everybody was scared of him again, and they had every right to be.

*I gotta do something.* And yet, what could I do? I couldn't drag him kicking and screaming into my living room. He was a grown man now. I couldn't make him come back, even though

I hated what he was doing. *He's gonna be okay*, I told myself. *He'll turn around again. He'll be back.*

When I saw him ride up to the corner gas station on his bike one night, I thought that moment might have come. I grinned at him. But TO didn't smile back.

"When are you coming back?" I asked him, trying not to seem desperate.

TO didn't look at me as he shook his head, his dreads hanging loose around his face. "No disrespect, Miss Diane, but I just don't believe in that peace thing no more."

His words didn't make sense. "What are you talking about? Why?"

"It's not working." He shrugged. "I done got older now. Things are different."

I wanted to prick him with my pen and fuss at him, tell him he was talking crazy and if he had any sense, he'd march back to KOB right then and there. But what good would that do? He wouldn't listen.

"TO, I'm here if you need me," I said, reaching out to touch his arm. "The house is always open."

"I'll see you around, Miss Diane," he said. He caught my eye. Somewhere in those brown eyes of his was the boy I knew, the boy I'd watched strut around the basketball court with a clipboard under his arm, handing out snacks and taking notes like his life depended on it. Deep down, he was still that same TO who puffed up with pride when I put him in charge of picking up trash or leading a search party. He was the same leader, the same kid I knew would bring dozens of other boys with him if he turned his life around.

*God, protect him*, I prayed as he rolled off on his bike. I'd heard the rumors. I knew there were boys out to get him.

"I'll see you, TO," I called out. And I really believed that I would.

At least a dozen young people were crammed in the van with me that October night in 2010. We were on our way back to my house after a youth antiviolence banquet. Rap music blared from our speakers, kids laughed at me and pretended to be embarrassed as I rapped at the top of my lungs.

As I slowed to a stop at the light at 115th and Michigan, I saw the red tape. Police tape. I'd seen it enough times to know it meant something bad had happened. My heart pounded as I turned down the music, listening. I looked out the window to see young people I recognized. They were screaming, running around, panicked looks plastered on their faces.

"What's going on, Miss Diane?" a boy called from the back of the van.

I looked at Aisha in the passenger seat, a sinking feeling gnawing in my stomach. "I don't know," I said. "Let's see what's happening."

I pulled the van into the first parking spot I could find and stepped outside, Aisha and a few of the kids right behind me. I stood glued to the sidewalk, and Aisha ran to a group of girls she recognized. Out of the corner of my eye, I saw two boys. TO's friends. They were crying, their hands on their faces. *No. No. No.* I thought.

"What's going on?" I screamed. I'm not sure who I was asking, but nobody responded. I needed somebody to tell me that all the ruckus was for nothing.

And then, I saw him. Across the street, lying on the sidewalk, was TO.

His dreads he'd dyed red were spread out on the pavement. I didn't have to walk any closer to see they were soaked with blood. TO was gone.

I felt the scream form deep in my body. My eyes squeezed shut, as if somehow I could unsee what I'd just seen. It didn't matter. The image was burned in my brain. I felt like I'd shed my skin on the sidewalk. I couldn't ever be the same person I was before I saw TO's body. Everything had changed.

*Why didn't I pull him off that bike? Why didn't I make him come back in the program? I could have saved him. I could have fixed this. If I can't save these kids, I might as well close my door and quit.*

"Ma!" Aisha's voice brought me back to reality. "We gotta get out of here."

I turned to see TO's cousins and other family racing down the sidewalk toward the red tape. Word had spread fast. It always does. I could hear boys roaring at one another, getting in each other's faces. It wouldn't be long before somebody threw a punch or pulled out a gun. When a young person is killed in our community, everybody knows to stay off the street. The gangs would be out looking for whoever did it, and you didn't want to be around when they found him.

"Everybody, get back in the van!" I shouted over the commotion. I had to get them back to my house safely. I couldn't lose another kid.

We jogged away from the fight breaking out near TO's body. We'd be safe in my house. Everybody else would live to see another day.

I lay awake most of the night. I couldn't close my eyes without seeing TO's blood-soaked dreads. The bottom had dropped out of my stomach. Vomiting would have been a relief. Anything to stop the pain. But I wasn't even granted that.

*I just don't want it to be true*, I thought. For so long, TO was trying. He was showing up to programming. He was going to school and doing his homework. He wanted more for his life. And now it was over. I was furious at TO's cousin. Why did he have to show up and ruin everything we'd worked for? Maybe TO would have kept on working hard and making good choices. Maybe TO would be alive.

But the person I always came back to was me. I didn't do enough. I should have tried harder. It was my fault he was dead.

James and Aisha told me over and over that I couldn't blame myself. "Ma, he was living defiled," Aisha said sadly. "His life was dirty. You couldn't have done anything else."

The kids filled me in on a whole other side to TO I'd never known. They told me TO and his cousin had been out shooting at people over on State Street. They told me he had a baby on the way, a baby who would now be another fatherless Roseland kid.

Nothing they said changed how I felt. TO had made some horrible choices. He had been walking the wrong path. But did that mean his life was worth any less? Did that mean he deserved what he got? I still believed that he deserved another chance. If only he were still alive, I wouldn't give up on him. I wouldn't order him to leave my house and never come back. Everybody has the potential to turn their life around.

I walked around for months with that sick feeling in my stomach. I felt like a complete failure. I wanted to quit. If I was being honest, I didn't want to risk hurting like this ever again. *God, what's the point?* I cried out. *Why am I doing this?*

*It's not working. It doesn't matter what I do. I couldn't save TO. What if I lose somebody else?*

But in those low moments, God was there. I felt His Spirit whispering to me in the stillness. *Those kids still need you*, I felt Him say. *They need you now more than ever.*

Somehow, I kept going. Even when I didn't want to. Every day, I opened my front door. I gathered boys and girls in mentoring sessions. I helped them with their homework. I cheered for them on the basketball court. Even so, I couldn't help wondering, does any of this matter? Is this working? Does anybody see it?

It turned out, I'd get my answer sooner than I thought.

# Hero

I sat up in bed panting, my heart pounding so hard I thought for sure James heard it too. I squinted at the digital alarm clock on the nightstand. It was three o'clock in the morning. I sighed.

Just a few minutes earlier, I'd finally laid my head on my pillow and closed my eyes. I'd prayed. I'd read articles on my iPad. I'd stared at the ceiling. For a moment, it looked like I might actually get some sleep. Sleep had never come easily to me, but since TO's death, I was lucky to get three hours a night. As soon as I drifted off tonight, though, images from earlier that afternoon came flooding back. Images of a young man in a white T-shirt holding a bat over his head. Images of me standing in front of him, my feet planted, daring him to hit me as my KOB kids took off running to my house.

The whole incident replayed in my head like a movie. At least fifteen kids and I were outside getting ready to head to the theater when three boys jumped out of a green SUV. They charged toward us, menacing looks plastered on their faces. Everybody ran when they noticed one of the boys held a bat. Everybody except me. My mind screamed over and over, *Don't run!*

In that moment, I wasn't some short lady in her fifties. Some kind of Holy Ghost boldness came over me as I stared down the guy with the bat. *I can't lose another kid*, I thought. *I'm not letting that happen.*

"You gonna hit me with that bat?" I asked him. He flinched, surprised. "You do whatever you gotta do, but I'm not running. What you're doing is wrong."

He slowly lowered the bat.

"These kids aren't trying to harm you all!" I hollered. None of the boys said a word as they jumped back in the SUV and hit the gas, the tires squealing down the road. It wasn't until the SUV had disappeared that my knees shook.

Sitting in my bed that night, the boy's glare still haunted me. *Diane, what are you doing?* I asked myself. *You could have been killed. Ain't nothing stopping that boy from knocking you upside the head.*

I looked at James snoring away next to me. No way I was telling him about that afternoon's little incident. Not unless I wanted to hear him fuss at me. I'd heard it all before, every time I did something stupid like jump in front of a gang member. "Diane! Why are you risking your life like that?" he always demanded. I didn't know how to tell him that I was scared to death of somebody else ending up like TO. That I still wondered how I could have stopped him from falling back into the violence. That guilt gnawed at my stomach every time I thought of him.

I leaned back into the mattress and winced. My lower back ached when my anxiety was high. No massages or doses of Advil could touch it. If it wasn't my back, it was my knees. Between the blood pressure medicine my doctor had prescribed me and the hours I spent running those kids all over town, my knees throbbed by the end of each day. Since the day I started KOB, I'd felt like a big kid. These days, though, my body went out of its way to remind me I was well on my way to becoming an old lady. Maybe I was getting too old for this. Maybe I couldn't handle the stress anymore. Maybe if I quit now, I wouldn't have to see the body of another kid I loved on the sidewalk.

*I can't keep doing this.*

I started more days than I liked to admit with that thought running through my mind. It was all too much. I was too old. It was too hard. And then, I just kept going. A kid would tell me that something I'd said made a difference, or I'd see a once-sullen gang member smiling and laughing with the other kids, and I couldn't stop. The Lord put me here. He brought me these kids. He made them listen to me. He wanted me to open my doors and help them when no one else would.

I couldn't walk away. And yet, I'd be lying if I said I wasn't tired. I'd been that way since the day TO was shot. Much as I knew deep down I was making a difference, I couldn't help but wonder if anyone noticed. If anyone thought my little program mattered.

It was August, the height of our summer basketball program, and I was getting ready to head outside with the kids when I heard the faint sound of my ringtone.

The woman's voice on the other end was faint under the roar of young people bouncing basketballs and trash talking. "Can you go somewhere private?" I heard her ask me. "This is CNN."

My ears perked up. CNN? By now I'd had my share of reporters knock on my door. I was used to seeing my face on the local TV stations or in the *Chicago Tribune*. But CNN? Now, that sounded like the big time to me.

I hollered that I'd be right there before stepping into the bedroom and closing the door behind me. "Okay, go ahead," I told the woman.

"I'm calling to inform you that you have been nominated for a CNN hero award," the woman said.

My legs felt weak. I sank onto the bed. "Really?" Who in the world would have nominated me for that?

"Yes, and we have chosen you for our top ten."

The room spun. I heard the words this woman had just said, but they didn't feel real. Surely she'd dialed the wrong number. She couldn't be talking about me. Tears welled in my eyes. I was honored beyond belief. Just getting a call like this was incredibly humbling. But a nagging voice in my head told me I didn't deserve it. I hadn't done anything worth celebrating. I should have a whole notebook filled up with names of young people who enrolled back in school, kids who went off to college, boys who landed jobs they'd only dreamed of. I hadn't accomplished anywhere near that. I felt like a fraud. And now, CNN was about to find out I wasn't nearly as great as someone apparently told them I was.

Before I could speak, the woman jumped in with the upcoming logistics. She told me I couldn't say a word to anybody about the award just yet. CNN would send a few crews out to shoot promo videos that they would air in September, when they planned to feature each nominee throughout the month. Until then, I had to keep it quiet.

It was all I could do to compose myself as I opened the bedroom door and walked into the living room. I wanted to scream and jump up and down. I felt like my skin would burst from holding in this secret. But I gave the lady at CNN my word. I had to honor it.

For three whole weeks, I kept my mouth shut. I was quieter than usual, afraid that if I talked too much, it might slip out. James eyed me suspiciously from time to time. “What’s going on with you?” he’d ask. “You acting like you’re hiding something.”

I didn’t lie. But I didn’t break my promise. “Something big is coming,” I just said mysteriously.

When I could finally tell everybody that CNN was sending cameras to shoot videos, the whole room of kids erupted into shouts. Not one of those kids was an avid CNN watcher, but that didn’t stop them from plotting out how they could get their fifteen minutes of fame.

“Don’t y’all do nothing special,” I told them, trying to settle them down. They were all chattering like a bunch of little kids hopped up on candy. “Just be yourselves.”

One boy folded his arms, frowning. “Miss Diane, what you gonna wear?”

“Yeah,” another chimed in. “You gonna dress up and wear your eyelashes?”

Everybody in the room laid out laughing. Never in my life did I think these boys noticed whether I showed up in a cute jogging suit and nice sneakers or ratty sweatpants and a do-rag. Apparently, I was wrong.

"Alright, alright, y'all." I rolled my eyes as I tried not to laugh. "Don't you worry. I'll bring it for the cameras."

I made sure I had a weave in my hair and long eyelashes on my eyelids when the first crew arrived. They were followed by two other crews, each of them staying for a few days. They rolled their cameras as I mentored kids, walked down the streets of Roseland, and answered questions in personal interviews. They asked me all about why I started KOB, my biggest success, and my biggest failures. They pulled kids aside to ask them what KOB meant in their lives.

Finally, when the crews had come and gone, my contact at CNN, Liz Fellinger, called to tell me that the promos would air the following week. She added that I could tell my family about my nomination.

James didn't understand at first when I told him the news. "What does that mean you're a CNN hero?" he asked. "Do you have to fly anywhere?"

It wasn't until I pulled up a video of the previous year's awards ceremony that his eyes lit up. He hugged me over and over again. "Ain't that something," he'd say, shaking his head. I couldn't stop smiling as I watched him call up his brothers, sisters, and every living aunt and uncle he could think of back in Mississippi, telling them all about the award. He sure had come a long way from the days of threatening to divorce me over selling the TV.

My mom and Aisha both screamed over the news. "I told you that you needed to do something with those kids!" my mom said. She probably called half of Chicago as she dialed up her friends and family to brag about me. And my daughter Apprecia confessed that she'd nominated me for the award.

My phone rang nearly off the hook the night my promo first aired. It seemed like everybody I'd ever met called me to squeal that they'd just seen me on CNN. My phone blew up with email notifications I'd never be able to get through.

I gushed and chattered and told everybody how honored I was, but none of it felt real. I felt like I was watching a video about somebody else. My brain couldn't take in the idea that my story was being displayed on TV screens around the country. It was too much.

So instead, I focused on one of the most exciting parts—the trip. Liz had told me CNN would fly me and two family members out to California for the awards ceremony in December. A trip to California in the middle of winter sounded like heaven. Chicago winters are brutal. They don't call it the Windy City for nothing. The icy wind whips down the street and cuts straight through your coat. I grinned as I imagined basking under the warm Hollywood sun, watching the palm trees sway in the gentle breeze.

I'd only been to California once to visit my brother in Englewood years before. My mom and sister had traveled with me on a Greyhound bus because we had been too nervous to fly. By the time we'd finally gotten off the bus, we were swollen up like balloons from sitting so long. No way I was making that mistake this time.

I knew without asking that James wouldn't be able to come. He isn't scared of much, but he draws the line at flying. To this day, he's still never flown. Instead, I went with the next two obvious choices—Aisha and my mom.

But it didn't seem right not to have the rest of my kids there cheering for me on one of the biggest nights of my life. My bank account was a little too light to swing flying out everybody. So I improvised. My KOB kids helped me sell donated bags of Snickers and Twizzlers and wash cars in the alley across the street until we'd raised more than $3,000, enough to buy train tickets for my three daughters and two sons who could make the trip.

I was practically living in a dream world. I couldn't stop imagining what the Ritz-Carlton hotel would look like or which stars I'd take selfies with on the red carpet. I pictured myself sitting in a plush red seat in the Shrine theater and seeing singers and actresses across the aisle from me. Sometimes I still had to pinch myself. I was nobody. Just Diane over on Michigan. And I was about to get the star treatment. It didn't seem possible.

Finally, the day came. I had my weave on and packed a little black, ruffled dress I'd bought from Le Club. I was ready. As ready as I'd ever be.

Aisha jittered with nervous energy the whole flight. As soon as we landed, we hit the street, taking a cab out to an open-air market and walking to Hollywood Boulevard, Aisha snapping photos every second. We gazed in all the fancy shops—Michael Kors, Gucci, all the famous names we'd seen in magazines. Once, I tapped Aisha's shoulder rapidly and whispered, "That's Harpo!" I'd recognize that man anywhere. It was Willard E. Pugh, who played Harpo in *The Color Purple*. He graciously took a picture with us and pretended not to notice how starstruck we were.

When we went back to the Ritz-Carlton and were ushered into our room, I had to hold back a squeal. It was the most beautiful room I'd ever seen, with a giant bed, a luxurious bathroom, and even a small kitchen. I'm a humble woman, but in that moment, I felt like I must be somebody. The lobby was a prime spot for star spotting too—lots of them were staying there for the CNN Hero ceremony. I saw Jermaine Jackson and Tommy Davidson, and I even took a picture with

Laura Dern. By the time my head hit the pillow that night, my cheeks hurt from grinning. I was geeked up and happier than a five-year-old at Disneyland. *If those young people back home could see me now.*

I was up early the next day, in time for a CNN driver to pick me up in a Mercedes and take me, Aisha, and my mom to the Shrine theater. He ushered us into the back of the theater, where he regaled us with the building's history and all the stars who had walked those same halls. Liz, my CNN contact, showed us our seats and explained that nominees would practice their speeches before sitting down for separate interviews.

For the next three hours, I listened to the stories of my fellow nominees. I met a man who repurposed old hotel soaps. A chef who served dinner seven days a week to kids at a Boys & Girls Club. A woman who connected South African kids suffering from AIDS and poverty to volunteer mentors all over the world through the internet. And a woman who provided free prenatal care from a little hut in Indonesia. By the time they were done, I wanted to drop what I was doing and go follow them. *What am I doing with these people?* I wondered. *My work is nothing compared to everybody else's.*

Liz told me a celebrity would introduce me that night at the ceremony. I begged her to tell me who my person was, but her lips were sealed. The rest of the day, I racked my brain trying to guess.

I had to be back at the theater early for hair and makeup. That alone was an experience. I felt like a queen as a makeup artist dabbed my face with highlighter and eyeshadow, and a stylist twisted my weave into a classy updo. I had to blink a few times when I looked in the mirror to make sure that was really me staring back in the glass.

My mom and Aisha oohed and aahed over my look when they met me in the green room. We snapped selfies and laughed together until somebody told us it was time to find our seats. *This is it*, I thought. *This is real.*

We whispered to one another as we watched stars like Sarah Jessica Parker walk into the theater. But when I saw Chaka Khan, I popped out of my seat. Her music was everything to me during a pivotal time in my life, when I had been newly divorced and trying to get back on my feet. I practically bowed down at her feet, I was so in awe of her.

"Get up!" she said to me, laughing.

Everybody hushed as the lights dimmed and the host took the stage. I'd seen awards shows my whole life on TV. Now, sitting in the audience, I felt like I was watching somebody else sit there.

Technically, only one of the ten nominees would be named the CNN Hero of 2011, but I was not even thinking about that. I'd already won just by being there, as cliché as that sounds. As I clapped and cheered for all the other nominees, only one thought nagged at me—who would be my presenter?

When I saw Ice Cube take the stage, I screamed. I knew before he opened his mouth that he was for me. I'd been a fan of his for years and always liked his music—the clean versions, anyway.

"There's a force in the city of Chicago," he began. "She moves through her beloved Roseland neighborhood in search of young people who've gone down the wrong path. When she finds them, she takes them by the hand, and with the roar of a lioness, she says, 'I will not give up on you.'"

I could feel tears welling up in my eyes and fought with all my might to keep them in. No way was I going to cry off these eyelashes and this full face of makeup.

The audience applauded as Ice Cube announced my name. I stood, my ruffled dress swishing around my knees as I walked. I don't wear heels often, but I'd picked out a pair just for this occasion. Now I prayed I'd remember how to walk in them as I made my way to the stage. *Don't fall, don't fall.*

The speech I'd practiced earlier that afternoon scrolled down a teleprompter. I stared at it, trying to catch my breath, clutching my little award. In that moment, I flashed back to that July day in 2003, when I'd stood at my window watching Aisha and her friends running around the block and felt deep in my soul that the Lord wanted me to walk out that door and do something with those kids. I had no idea then the path that lay ahead of me when I put one foot in front of the other. The joys. The triumphs. The complete heartbreak. I certainly hadn't pictured myself walking onto a stage at the Shrine theater, spotlights shining in my eyes. The spotlight didn't motivate me to keep going. It didn't erase the pain of TO's death or the stress of keeping the peace between rivals or the frustration of watching a kid turn back to the gangs. But I had to admit, that recognition felt good. I felt seen. I felt noticed. No longer invisible.

And then I remembered the teleprompter.

"I go to bed at three or four in the morning. I get up at six or seven. I'm always excited. I know something good is gonna happen today because some kid is gonna say, 'Thank you, Miss Diane.' Some parent won't have to bury their child. All because of what we have done. Some father is gonna be proud."

I was supposed to stick to the script. The producer made that very clear. But I couldn't help myself. I had to get in one last thought.

"Please don't give up on our young people," I pleaded. "Please care about them. Please love them. I needed it, and so did you. Thank you."

I could hear the audience applaud and cheer as I walked backstage. Somebody told me Anderson Cooper had tweeted that I had all of them crying backstage. Liz pulled me aside for one last interview and introduced me to Ice Cube. As I shook his hand, I could see his eyes shining with tears.

"If I had somebody like you when I was growing up, things might have been different," he said.

I couldn't comprehend that night. My brain wouldn't let me. I felt like I was hovering above the theater, watching myself take it all in. One thought repeated itself over and over. *This will change everything*, I thought. *This will change KOB. Everybody will see what we do. They'll value the young people we serve too.*

I had no idea just how quickly that would happen.

CHAPTER SIXTEEN

# The Floodgates Open

I felt like I flew home from California on a cloud. Any thoughts of quitting, any doubts about whether I was making a difference, had evaporated into thin air. Being honored as a CNN Hero wasn't validation. It was a reminder. A reminder of the calling God had given me, of the honor it was to be trusted with these young people who looked to me for help, of the joy in seeing their lives change. I was on fire.

Even though I didn't win the top CNN Hero award, the network still sent me home with a $50,000 check. My mind raced with everything I could do for the kids with that kind of cash. I had a plan for every cent even before I deposited it in the bank. I wanted new computers for the kids to do their homework—we were still using the old dinosaurs I'd bought with the money from selling James's TV. I wanted printers. I wanted a fifteen-passenger van to load up even more kids and roll to rallies, block parties, and out-of-town trips. When a kid needed clothes or shoes, I wanted to drive them to the mall and buy them the best. I didn't believe in only giving scraps to kids in need. They deserved better than that. In the past, that had always come at my own expense. I'd use any spare cash I had to buy a warm coat or shoes that would last. Once, when two boys hadn't eaten in over a day, I took them to McDonald's with maybe $72 in my pocket. Those boys ate up almost every dime I had. Teenage boys can eat. I just let them get at it. They needed it more than I did. I never saw it as a sacrifice. It was something I wanted to do. But now I had some help.

CNN had also set up an account where people who saw my story on TV could donate online. I hadn't expected much to come from that. I'd accepted online donations for years and only saw maybe $100 a week, and that was on a good week. I doubted anything would change.

But it turned out I'd majorly underestimated the power of a national audience. Suddenly, money flowed in. I'm talking upward of $500 every day. I had to refresh the page and do a double take just to make sure it was real.

It couldn't have come at a better time. In the midst of the CNN chaos, the moment I thought would never happen finally came. Kids Off the Block got a grant to move into a building down the street. After years of squeezing everybody into three rooms of my little house, we'd have 2,500 square feet of office space all to ourselves. I was over-the-moon excited but probably not as excited as James. That man was thrilled to get his castle back and reclaim his rightful spot as king.

The kids helped us haul every last computer, printer, amp, and chair into the new center. We tacked pictures and awards on the blue-and-white walls and slid desks and tables across the blue tile floor. A donated church pew sat by the front door where parents could wait for their kids after programming. We lined the south side of the building with computers and printers and found a spot for a big conference table somebody had donated to us, where I envisioned us talking out problems in mentoring sessions. Long folding tables on one end of the building were covered with art supplies. James built a cubicle-sized music studio in the middle of the wide-open space, with walls covered in soundproof foam so nobody would be disturbed when they recorded. I even got my own office. It was barely big enough to hold two chairs in front of my desk, but it might as well have been executive-sized. I felt like I'd really made it every time I sat down to review sign-in sheets or create basketball schedules in peace.

With more space came more opportunities. We didn't have to limit ourselves to mentoring, homework help, and music. Now we had computer training. We had a representative from a job-placement business visiting us three times a week to teach kids about job applications and résumés. We had art classes and dance programs with space for all the girls to spread their arms and kick their legs up.

As much as the move was a blessing, it was also a leap of faith. KOB didn't own its new home. We just rented it. A grant paid our rent for six months, but after that, we were on our own. That meant every single month, I may have to beg, scream, and holler just to hand our landlord a check on time. The Lord always blessed us. Somehow we got by. Thanks to the CNN exposure, we had all these donations from strangers that would more than cover the bill. It was another burden off my shoulders, one less thing to worry about.

A lot of these donors assumed I took a salary, that more donations meant I could get a raise. Everybody was shocked when they learned I didn't get paid. I still don't. Providing for the kids is my first priority. There was always something they needed, another opportunity I could get for them if only we had the money. I wasn't worried about myself. James and I would get by. The Lord always made sure of that. But the donors looked at me like I was crazy.

One of those donors was a lady named Donna Baker. She called me one day after seeing me on CNN. "Oh my gosh!" I heard her exclaim when I said hello. "You answer your own phone?" She cackled so loudly I had to laugh with her.

Donna was a white woman from the suburbs, but she told me she used to live in Roseland back when she was in high school. She remembered how beautiful it used to be and told me how heartbroken she was to see how far the neighborhood had fallen. She asked me all kinds of questions, too, wanting to know who my husband was and how long I'd been married and practically my whole life story. It seemed like every other phrase out of her mouth was "Oh my gosh!" She was blunt and direct, and I liked her right away. She didn't just want to talk. She wanted to help.

"I want to come out there and see what you're doing," she said.

I'd heard that from supporters many times. They never followed through. But Donna did. She and her husband, Bobby, pulled up to the center one day with giant bags of candy for the kids. If they weren't sure about her when they first laid eyes on her, they certainly changed their minds when she handed out that candy.

Donna had told me she was short, and she wasn't kidding. She couldn't have been taller than four foot three. But this lady was a powerhouse. She marched into the center and surveyed the space, nodding absently. By the time I'd shown her around, she had a whole list of supplies we needed. Then she went out and got them right then and there.

Her husband, meanwhile, never came out of the music studio. Once he found out we had one, that was it for him. It turned out he was a musician and used to play clarinet with Miles Davis. Zeek and a few other boys kept him busy listening to tracks and adjusting mixes.

My stomach hurt from laughing by the time I waved goodbye to Donna and Bobby. Something about her take-charge attitude connected with my spirit. I knew she was going to be important to me for years to come.

Donna promised she'd be in touch. True to her word, she called almost every week to find out how we were doing and what we needed. She mailed checks and sent supplies regularly. Over time, she became more than just a donor. She became a friend. I smiled every time I saw her name on my screen when the phone rang. On paper, we didn't have much in common. She was a staunch atheist, while I was a proud follower of Jesus. She was well-to-do, while I had to get on my knees and pray just to pay my bills every month. She lived in the suburbs; I lived in the city. And yet, somehow we just clicked. She told me she admired me and my work, but to me, she was the one who was inspirational. She'd been sick most of her life with illnesses I'd never heard of and couldn't pronounce. I knew she spent more time than she'd like stuck in bed, waiting for a new medication to kick in and get her back on her feet. I respected her tenacity, her determination, and her commitment to help the kids of KOB.

And she wasn't the only helper my appearance on CNN had brought to me. For years, I'd leaned on James and my mom to help me keep an eye on the kids and run my programs. Now I had new volunteers. There were Tasia and Bree, who worked with the media, hung up flyers, and talked to people in the community to maximize our exposure. There was Ruby, who kept our books in order. Dominique, who acted as my community liaison. Trey, who ran our mentoring program and lined up volunteers. Zeek, who had come so far from his bad-attitude days that he now rode around the community talking to young people and bringing them to the program.

Aisha was twenty-one by now and living on her own. She was out helping people, too, working as a youth coordinator for Safety Net Works. But she still stopped by almost every day to help me and see what we needed at KOB. If I said, "Nothing," she put her hand on her hip and stared at me. "Ma!" she'd holler in that voice that meant I'd better tell her something or she'd come up with something to do on her own.

By now, I'd learned how to delegate. I had to. Between our league's thirtysomething basketball teams and the seventy-five-plus kids in and out of the program every day, I had to come to grips with the fact that I couldn't do it all. I had to relinquish some control. That wasn't easy. When Aisha and Tasia told me they would take care of something, my insides tensed up. If they were leaving to pick up food, I'd think, *but you don't know what they really love to eat like I do!* Or I'd convince myself that no one else could manage registration like I could. I thought I was doing what was best for KOB. I did some research online and discovered something called "founder's syndrome." One look at the description and I knew that's what I was doing. So when I caught myself falling back into that old trap, I could recognize it and stop myself. And if I didn't, Aisha would roll her eyes at me and shout, "Ma! We got it!"

With all the recognition, donations, and volunteers, I thought my battle for legitimacy was over. All I'd have to do was point to the CNN Hero clip about me and say, "See what we're doing over here? If it's good enough for CNN, it's good enough for you!"

But instead, I found myself bending over backward trying to prove myself even more. I wasn't just "Diane over on Michigan" to my community anymore. I was "Diane the CNN Hero." They walked into the center with their arms crossed, expecting to be impressed. The trouble was, I wasn't any more impressive than I ever had been.

It only got worse when I won a BET Shine a Light award. The kids had been excited about the CNN award, but when they found out about BET, you'd have thought I'd been knighted. This was some hood fame. I had to prove myself all over again. And the exposure didn't stop—one of the biggest instances, I didn't see coming. It started as just a TV news story. I was busy in the center one day when two white people—a girl and a guy—walked in.

"Are you Diane Latiker?" one of them asked. They told me they were from LA 40 Productions, and somebody had recommended that they do a story about me. "Would you be willing to let us hang with you for a couple of days?"

After I said yes, they told me they'd be back the next day. They opened the center's front door the next day with a short, middle-aged white guy in tow.

"This is Steve," the woman said. "Would it be okay if he volunteered with you while we're taping?"

"Sure. Hey, Steve!" I said. I never said no to a volunteer, and Steve seemed nice enough.

The kids and I were about to head outside to paint and clean a viaduct. Steve helped us gather up our equipment and introduced himself to the kids as we walked through the front door. I didn't take him for much of a handyman—he had this look about him like he hadn't done much manual labor. But he jumped right in like he'd worked with us from day one, laughing and joking with the kids and suggesting what we ought to do next. *This guy's alright*, I thought. Cameras recorded our every move—footage for the story, the people from LA 40 told us.

Steve was back the next morning, and the next, working his tail off and asking the kids questions about their parents or school or what it's like living in Roseland. But as the days went by, I stood back and frowned. Those cameras that followed us around weren't pointed at the kids or the viaduct they were painting. They were pointed right at Steve.

I have never been known as a woman who keeps my mouth shut. If I feel something, I let it out. So when I saw a producer walking around our project, I marched up to him in a huff. "You told me you were doing a story on the kids, right?" I said, not in the nicest tone. "But every time I turn around, the camera is on Steve."

He assured me the story would focus on the kids, and I went back to work. Still, every time I looked at a camera, the lens was zoomed in on Steve. After a few days, I'd had it.

"That's it," I snapped, setting down my paintbrush and standing up. "I'm tired of this." I walked straight back to the center, muttering to myself the whole way. "These people are getting on my nerves. This story should be about the kids. They're the most important."

"Diane," a voice said in my ear. "We can hear you."

In my frustration I'd completely forgotten about the microphone strapped to my body and the earpiece in my ear. These producers had heard every bit of my little rant.

I was too frustrated to be humiliated. "Oh really?" I shot back. "Well, hear this." I snatched off the microphone and threw it down as I walked into the center.

The producers rushed inside in a flash, their faces twisted with concern. "What's wrong?" they all asked at once, as if they hadn't heard my list of grievances. "We'll do better, we'll do better, we promise!"

I swallowed my pride and returned to the viaduct. We finished painting, and the kids and I headed back to the center. I still couldn't shake the feeling that something was going on that they weren't telling me, but since I couldn't put my finger on it, I figured all I could do was let it go.

But that evening, as I sat with my mom on my porch, we saw Steve walking down the street, heading nowhere in particular. Three cameras followed him as he noticed us on the porch and waved. He didn't cross the street but kept on walking.

"Something is wrong here," I said quietly, keeping my eyes glued on Steve.

"What do you think it is?" my mom asked.

I shook my head. "I don't know. But why would those cameras be following him?"

When my phone rang that night, it was Steve. He didn't say a word about the cameras but had a different request.

"Can you have everyone meet me at the lot tomorrow?" he asked. "I'm heading out of town, and I wanted to say goodbye to all the kids."

The next morning the kids were at my house around nine—they were already planning to arrive early because we were working on summer projects around the neighborhood. When I told them Steve was leaving that day, they dissolved into whines and protests. I knew they liked him, but I hadn't realized how much.

We headed across the street to the lot and waited, the morning sun just starting to warm the asphalt. It wasn't hot yet, but I could tell it would be soon if Steve didn't get a move on.

The kids grinned and waved when they noticed Steve walking to the lot. But they froze when they heard a loud trampling. We all looked at one another, our eyes wide. "What in the world?" I asked.

Before anybody could answer, at least forty people, all dressed in black, rushed onto the lot holding giant cameras. They looked like they could have been dressed in tactical gear for all I knew. *I was right*, I thought. *Something is up. This dude has been lying to us*. I stared at Steve. "What is going on here?" I demanded.

Steve smiled. "Diane, I have something to tell you. I'm not who I said I was."

"What, your name's not Steve?" a boy behind me yelled.

He laughed. "No, my name is Steve."

He paused for a moment. We all leaned in, anxious to hear this guy's big reveal, whatever it was.

"Actually, I'm part of ABC's *Secret Millionaire*," he said.

My jaw nearly hit the ground. I'd imagined something was going on behind the scenes, but this wasn't exactly what I'd had in mind.

"You're . . . you're a millionaire?"

"Yes," he said simply. "And I'm really impressed with what you guys have done. I want to help you grow."

By now my hands were cupped over my mouth, as if they could hold back the sobs. I couldn't believe this was happening. For years, I'd dreamed about somebody dropping out of the sky and extending a helping hand. I'd written to Oprah more times than I could count, thinking she could be my guardian angel or something. But to experience it in real life was more than I could have imagined.

Steve reached into his pocket and pulled out a piece of paper. I knew it was a check. *Is this guy really giving me $10,000?* I thought. My head spun thinking about all we could do with that kind of money.

He handed me the check and I dove in for a hug. Then I took a closer look at the check. I started counting the zeros. Three, four, five. This check was for $100,000.

I screamed and jumped up and down like I was a Publishers Clearing House winner on Super Bowl Sunday. "Oh my gosh! Oh my gosh!" I hollered over and over. I was in shock, still trying to comprehend what this man was doing for us.

And he wasn't done. "I've got something else for you," he said. Two trucks pulled into the lot out of nowhere, and men unloaded boxes of Mac computers and printers. When a guy carried out a box holding a big-screen TV, James and I laid out laughing. I'd forgotten that I'd told Steve about selling James's TV.

"Don't you touch this TV!" James said as everybody laughed.

Every single one of us cheered and hugged one another. It was a celebration like I'd never experienced.

And he still wasn't done. A giant truck roared down the alley as Steve pulled out a poster. He unrolled it to reveal the most beautiful basketball court I'd ever seen.

"I'm going to build you a new basketball court," he said.

If the kids were excited before, they were out-of-their-minds ecstatic now. They nearly tackled Steve, hugging him so hard that I was worried for his back.

I watched those boys trash talk one another and brag about who was going to dunk on whom and who was going to score the most points. *These kids are gonna have the best*, I thought. After all this time of refusing to give them scraps and giving them the best that I could afford, someone had stepped in to do me one better. Someone was giving them world-class computers and a world-class basketball court, helping me provide world-class programs.

Somebody saw us. Somebody believed we were doing important work. I'd shouted it from the rooftops since the beginning, always feeling like nobody heard. And now, somebody did. Lots of somebodies. I still didn't feel like I deserved any of it, but it sure was helpful.

*God, I don't know why You're using me like this*, I prayed. *But thank You.*

CHAPTER SEVENTEEN

# Battlefield Outside My Door

Once the media came knocking on my door, it never truly stopped. I'd opened a door I couldn't close. Newspapers called me for a quote when another shooting rocked the city, or reporters dropped by our Feed a Teen or Christmas party events. CNN checked in on me now and then to update my story. *Essence* magazine even came calling, featuring me in a list of "Ten Things We're Talking About." Local TV news cameras were a regular fixture around here, so much that the kids barely even blinked when they noticed a crew setting up. Everybody knew me as Miss Diane, the lady over on Michigan, the lady who can help.

I didn't start any of this for the media attention, but it came with some benefits. I'd see new faces walk through the center door with each news article and mention in the media. Other nonprofits stopped dismissing me—at least for the most part—as some old lady who didn't know what she was doing. KOB was recognized as a force to be reckoned with, a peacekeeper in Roseland.

But attention, it turns out, is a double-edged sword. Not everybody who watched me on TV liked what they saw. Not everybody was happy about me helping any gang member who walked through my door. By sharing my story with the world, I was essentially sticking a target on my own back. I was stepping into a battle without even knowing it.

For as long as gangs have ruled the streets of Roseland, certain groups have hated one another. Some of those rivalries are based on arguments from so long ago that nobody can really remember who started them or what they were about. And sometimes, they're all about race. I've known since the day I started KOB that the black gangs are always getting into it with the Hispanic gangs. It wasn't just one gang—it was all of them.

For the most part, the black gangs don't live side-by-side with the Hispanic gangs. If they want to ride by somebody's house or retaliate for some wrongdoing, they have to cross into the other group's territory. There's a definite battle line. And that battle line just happened to be right by my house. The gas station just across the way was the only gas station in the area, the only place where anybody could pick up bags of Hot Cheetos or bottles of pop. That meant Hispanic boys who lived up the hill behind my house would run into boys from the black gangs right there on Michigan.

Now, my door has always been open to anybody: black, white, brown, any color. But the Hispanic boys looked at me and saw a woman helping their enemy. They watched black boys go riding by their people and come right to my house and believed I was in on it, that I was some kind of gang mother. I tried over the years to reach out to boys in the Hispanic gangs. I met with gang leaders and told them I wanted to help them too. Once, when a big brown building on the corner was turned into a shelter for homeless youths, we invited the mostly Hispanic boys there to play basketball with us. Basketball had overcome so many gang rivalries in the past; I thought it could heal this one too. But the gangs weren't having it. Eventually I had to stop begging them to come and focus on helping the kids who were willing to take it.

I'd accepted that these boys didn't like me. Our paths didn't cross often, and for the most part, they left me alone. Meanwhile, I smiled and spoke passionately for the TV cameras, not knowing that each appearance made them angrier. Their rage had reached a boiling point, and I had no idea. Until it was in my face.

My mom and I were sitting on her porch talking, like we normally do most days. We leaned back in our plastic lawn chairs, fanning ourselves from the summer heat as I filled her in on the latest drama at KOB. At first, I didn't pay attention to the young man riding up on his bike. Most boys don't have cars, so they use their bikes to get around the neighborhood. And then I saw it. Right in his hand, gleaming in the sun, was a .45. A gun. And he was heading straight toward us.

My stomach dropped as the boy drove his bike in circles on the sidewalk, screaming at us in broken English. "You're helping them!" he shouted, a menacing snarl on his face. "We're gonna kill all of them. Stop helping them!"

I kept my eyes locked on the boy, waiting for him to stop waving the gun, ready to throw myself on the ground and duck from flying bullets. My mom craned her neck toward the sky and clasped her hands together. "The blood of Jesus!"

she cried out to God. "The blood of Jesus!" Then, without any explanation, the boy rode off without firing a shot.

An SUV rolled up. In a flash, I saw somebody roll down the window. I saw a blurry face, a hand clutching a green bottle. I heard my mom gasp as the bottle crashed onto the bottom step, followed by the explosive thud of a brick. Green glass shattered into a million pieces, glimmering in the sun as it covered the sidewalk.

Neither of us moved until the SUV disappeared. For a moment, I wasn't sure if I could breathe. I've heard about bottles thrown on porches and boys riding up on bicycles, but I'd always been immune. I was never a target. Now I couldn't get the look on that boy's face out of my mind. There was hatred in his eyes, a cold, dead hatred. I knew we were lucky that all we had to deal with was a broken bottle. It could have been so much worse.

"I'm sorry you had to experience that," I said to my mom. I wanted to say so much more, but no words sounded right.

She shrugged. "God had us."

I should have known better than to worry. My mom isn't the type of person who scares easily. I thought of our early days in Roseland when she lived with us. In those days, a notorious gang lived right next door. We had hit the deck day after day, terrified out of our minds, as somebody rode by with their windows down, the earsplitting, high-pitched crack of gunshots ringing out in the street. Anytime I declared I'd had it and was ready to move, my mom wouldn't hear of it.

"We gonna pray them out," she said. "The Lord will take care of it."

Her faith was steady even as the drive-bys kept coming, even when we felt like prisoners in our own home. "God has us," she'd say when my own knocking knees and chattering teeth got in the way of my faith. So we kept falling on our knees. We kept crying out to God. And we wrote letters to the mayor to let him know what was happening.

Then one day, we awoke to complete silence. The feds had slipped in overnight and raided the whole place. Every last gang member was gone. The drive-bys stopped. Mom was right. God had us all along. He did then. And He would now.

Much as I believed God had us, I also believe faith without works is dead. I knew I had to take action, and the best thing I could do was call the police. Commander Ball sent some officers over to my street and also to question boys who'd been targeting us. One officer reported back to me that several families felt I was harboring gang members who were out to get them.

"That's not my intent at all," I said, pleading with him. "If you can, please let them know that KOB is open to them too. But I can't have them threatening my mom, or me."

For a while, I thought that one call to the police was enough. Months went by without a single incident. I didn't forget what had happened. It was still there, lurking in the back of my mind. But I had to keep going. I couldn't live in fear. But I knew it wasn't over.

One night they attacked Jamal. He was twenty-one by then, still coming to KOB. His grandma needed some groceries, so he'd stopped at a corner store to pick up eggs, milk, and bread for her. Those eggs spilled all over the railroad tracks as boys hidden in the alley fired at him. Jamal was shaken up but thankfully not hurt. Still, I was furious that these boys had attacked Jamal all because they were mad at me. *This has got to stop*, I thought. *Somebody's got to do something*.

I marched straight to Commander Ball's office and told him the city had to do something about the railroad tracks by my house. Anybody who crossed them was an easy target for somebody who wanted to hide in the alley. I had to wait a few months, but the city finally installed a steel fence by the alley, too high for anybody to climb. It was a start, but I knew it wasn't enough. We weren't safe. Not yet.

It was already dark outside as James and I kicked back to relax after programming. He was watching some old-school rerun of his beloved *Sanford and Son* while I flipped through news articles on my iPad. The only way I could stomach James's beloved sitcoms was if I ignored them, but at least it meant we got a little time together. Time together still didn't come easily, even though I didn't have kids sleeping at my house anymore or staying all hours of the night.

I jumped out of my chair when my phone rang. My phone never rings at night with good news. When I saw DaJuan's number on the screen, I picked it up.

"Miss Diane, there's a gang surrounding your house." His voice was slow, deliberate, as if he wasn't quite sure what to do with the information.

His words didn't compute. Surely he was looking at somebody else's house. This was just a normal night. My heart beat faster as I remembered the boy on the bicycle, the kids shooting at Jamal from the alley. "What?"

"I just drove by," he said. "They're out there."

I suddenly felt like somebody must be crouching in the corner. "Where are they?"

"Just peek out your window."

I turned to face my window. All that stood between me and whoever was outside was a thin layer of glass and a burgundy curtain. I didn't want to look. I didn't want to know. Maybe if I didn't see them, it wouldn't be real. But I couldn't just pretend they weren't there. I pulled back the edge of the curtain, just enough to sneak a look.

And there they were. In the second I dared to look out the window, I counted seven of them. All of them standing right by my house, so close I could have seen the designer logo on the back of their jeans. All of them were dressed in black hoodies.

Quickly, I dropped the curtain and leaned against the wall. I thought my dinner was about to come back up. *What are they doing here?* I thought, racking my brain about any news article or incident that would have riled up this gang. *They ain't here for scenery. Lord Jesus, what am I gonna do?*

My eyes fell on James, still sitting in his chair, oblivious to the world beyond his little TV show.

"James," I said quietly. "Turn out the light, and get on the floor."

He looked up at me with surprise. "For what?"

I swallowed and spoke in the calmest voice I could muster. "Because there's a gang outside. They're surrounding our house and I don't know why."

We flipped off the lights and nearly belly flopped onto the floor, our noses on the linoleum. The room was pitch-black except the glow of my cell phone as I dialed the police station. In the stillness, I could hear somebody moving in the bushes just outside the window. Somebody muttered in a low voice. I felt like every ounce of blood in my body rushed to my head as we waited. I've seen plenty of boys pull guns in my days. I've stood at the end of a barrel without batting an eye. But there in my house, lying in the dark, I was terrified. I looked at James, feeling overwhelmed with guilt. He was just as terrified as I was. I wanted to fix it, to rip the target off my back. But I felt helpless. Here I've been trying to help kids, no matter where they came from or what they've done. I would have helped these boys too—these boys now surrounding my house. But they wouldn't hear of it. They only saw me as an enemy.

Suddenly, a bright light cut through the cracks in my curtains. James and I looked at one another, confused. I crawled toward the window and pulled back the shade. A police spotlight just about burned through my retinas. I stood up and sighed. Everybody in Roseland knows the last thing you want is the police to shine their spotlight. It doesn't solve anything. All it does is send whoever's bothering you scattering, without giving the police a chance to arrest or question anybody. I saw figures racing down Michigan Avenue.

I'd made up my mind not to tell the kids, but word had already spread. DaJuan apparently didn't waste any time. By the next night, just about everybody who walked into KOB was heated, talking about what they were going to do about it.

"No, no, no," I protested. "You're just gonna make it worse. We're not gonna fall into that."

"Miss Diane, we can't let them get away with that!" Jamal shot back.

"Well, technically, they didn't do anything this time," I said, trying to squash the situation. "They just surrounded my house. But then they left."

Nobody told me they went out and retaliated. I didn't hear about anybody riding by somebody's house or any alley gunfights. But I wondered. I still do.

I wish the whole situation had been wrapped up with a neat, pretty bow. More than anything, I wanted resolution, a way to stop worrying that I'd get another late-night call or that another boy would ride up on his bike with a gun. The worries never stopped. Honestly, today, I still wonder. I don't know what made them stop. I don't know if they'll be back. Gang violence is like that. It doesn't make sense. It doesn't have a rhyme or reason. It doesn't have a tidy ending. It's messy. It's complicated. Looking back, I have to hand the credit to God. He's the only reason James and I were safe. He's the only reason the gang stopped coming around. He's the reason I'm still here.

All along, I trusted that the battlefield was outside the walls of KOB. I knew some of these kids were still in gangs. I knew they ran around getting into it with this person or that. But from what I understood, it only went so far. There was a limit. I thought I could intervene before they crossed that line. If I just said the right things or spent enough time with them, they'd stay out of trouble. I kept on believing that, even after I lost TO. Maybe I clung to it even harder. I was on a mission to rescue these kids. We were fighting a life-and-death battle here, and it was up to me to protect them.

And then, Donnie showed up. Donnie had been with KOB for a while. Back when we recorded the video for "Save a Teen," he was there, posing in the background. He'd never been as open as some of the other kids, and he certainly never clung to me like Jamal or DaJuan did. But I thought I knew him. I thought I understood what made him tick.

Normally Donnie was laid back and chill. On one particular night, though, his eyes darted around erratically, like he was on high alert. He pulled his hoodie closer to his body and tugged the hood over his head.

When I answered the door, he pushed right past me and into the house. I hadn't even had a chance to say hello before he sat down in my living room. His breathing was heavy, like he'd just finished the 100-yard dash. *No way this kid been running for the track team*, I thought.

"Donnie, what's going on?" I asked, worried. "Why you looking like that?"

Donnie pulled down his hoodie and rumpled his hair absently. He looked frazzled, anxious. "I did something stupid, Miss Diane."

I tried to comprehend what "stupid" meant to him. *Oh, boy, what have you done?* I wondered. I knew what some of these kids did when I wasn't around. If they thought drive-bys and fights made sense, I wasn't sure if I wanted to know what he considered stupid.

"Well," I said slowly, "you need to go home and take care of yourself."

I didn't want to ask him outright what he had done. I sure dropped plenty of hints. He wasn't having it. He didn't say much at all, just listened and nodded along.

Finally, he jumped to his feet and pulled on a backpack. "I'll see you, Miss Diane," he said quietly.

I sank into a chair as the screen door slammed shut behind him. *Lord in heaven, what did this boy do? Why did he just tell me this?*

I was still in the living room wondering what to do when I heard voices out on the sidewalk. "Dude, what's wrong?" somebody said. I recognized the voice right away as DaJuan.

"Man, I did something stupid." It was Donnie. Still outside. Still saying the same old thing.

"Well, what did you do?" DaJuan pressed him.

For a moment, nobody spoke. I held my breath, trying not to make a sound. Was he finally going to say it out loud?

"This dude kept coming up in my building," I heard Donnie say. "I told him to stop, but he be tripping. I can't have him disrespecting me like that."

Another pause. "So what did you do?" DaJuan asked again.

"I took care of it."

"You shot him?"

"Yeah, man, I shot him."

Goosebumps covered my skin. I literally felt like my blood ran cold. This boy had just been in my house. He'd sat right next to me. And he'd just shot somebody minutes earlier. What if somebody came looking to attack him in my house? What if the police showed up and thought I was harboring a criminal? I could feel my body shaking.

"Did anybody see you?" DaJuan asked.

Donnie paused again. "There was a crowd around. This dude was laying on the ground, like, oh please, don't shoot me," he said, mimicking his victim in a high-pitched voice. "And I shot him."

My fear turned to rage. Donnie had been in my program for years. I poured my soul into this boy, trying to keep him on the straight and narrow. And now he goes and gets a gun, and not only shoots somebody but does it to a kid lying on the ground begging for his life.

From day one, I've believed no kid is too far gone. Anybody can be saved if they want it. But this was my breaking point. I can't save a kid who doesn't want to be saved. I can't save a kid who's dead set on violence.

I knew I had to do the right thing. And I knew I was letting Donnie go. I wouldn't visit him in prison. I wouldn't write letters. I was done. Much as I didn't want to let go, I had to. And that hurt. It was like seeing TO dead on the sidewalk all over again.

*You can't save everyone, Diane*, I felt the Lord telling me. I knew He was right. But I felt like something inside me broke.

# CHAPTER EIGHTEEN

# We're Worth It

"James!"

I shouted as loudly as I could. I'd just sprinted from the KOB center down the street and back to my house as fast as my legs could carry me. I needed James to see what I had just seen. To tell me if it was really as bad as I thought it was.

James ran out of the bedroom, his forehead furrowed. "Diane, what's wrong?"

I leaned on the back of a folding chair for a moment and tried to catch my breath. "It's the center," I managed to say between gasps. "The roof caved in."

James sighed. "I'll get my tool belt." What exactly he thought he'd do with a hammer and screwdriver, I didn't know, but I didn't argue.

We rushed back to the center and pushed open the door. There it was, just as bad as I'd remembered it. Right in the middle of the 2,500-square-foot room was a hole in the ceiling the size of my living room. What had once been a thick plaster ceiling looked like it had exploded all over the room. Plaster was everywhere, covering the computers, printers, tables, even the music studio. I looked up and saw straight to the sky.

James shook his head, his hand on his hip. "I knew this was gonna happen."

I used every ounce of restraint not to smack him upside the head. My pen would have come in handy right about then. "Then why didn't you fix it?" I snapped.

"Hey now," he said, holding up his hands like I was the police. "Don't go blaming me."

"I know, I know." I mentally calculated the damage. Just cleaning up the plaster would be a major undertaking. And our landlord wasn't exactly in a hurry to fix any repairs I'd called him about in the past.

*Lord, what are we gonna do?* I thought. *These kids are counting on me to be here for them. What am I supposed to do if I don't have a place for them to come?* I didn't want to close, not even for a day. What if the kids showed up and our door was locked? They might think we closed up for good, and they might never come back. I couldn't let that happen.

Calling the landlord didn't make me feel better. My heart sank when I heard his tried-and-true line. "I'll get to it," he said, ignoring me when I pressed him for a firm date.

James barely looked at me as I told him what the landlord said. He was too busy staring up at that hole, feeling the cool October breeze.

"I think I can fix it," he said confidently.

"Fix it?" I looked at him like he was crazy. "The roof is gone too. How you gonna fix that?"

"Well, maybe I can patch the ceiling enough to hold us," he said. "Just enough to get through until the landlord takes care of it."

I rolled my eyes. It was going to be a cold day in you-know-where before my landlord showed up. I didn't know what good it would do to fix the ceiling when the roof let every ounce of rain and snow inside. But once James sets his mind on something, nobody's going to tell him otherwise.

Together, with the help of a few volunteers and KOB kids, we cleaned up the plaster. James hauled his ladder and tools over to the center and patched the ceiling. For two weeks, we kept trying. We pretended we weren't freezing our tails off as the cold autumn wind cut through James's sad little patch. We kept up our mentoring sessions, the musicians kept recording, the dancers kept dancing. But every day, that patch looked a little more rickety. And every day, the landlord didn't show up.

A thought lurked in the back of my brain. *This hole might very well never get fixed. We might need a new building.*

By the end of two weeks, I'd had enough. This center wasn't safe. If the roof had fallen in once, it could do it again, and next time could be even worse.

"That's it," I declared after James had to march in with his tool belt once again. "We're outta here. We're moving back into our house."

It was a no-brainer. I wasn't upset about losing my personal space or moving backward to the old days of KOB. This was just what we had to do. Sure, we wouldn't have much space, but I'd made it work before. I could do it again. Besides, it was only temporary, I told myself. Just until we find a new building. We'd be out in a month or two.

James, however, wasn't too keen. This man enjoyed being king. He loved not having to worry about a kid snacking on the leftovers he stashed in the fridge or breaking our new sofa.

"Why are you doing this again?" he asked. "Just close for a couple months until we're able to figure this out."

"Because I'm making progress with these kids," I protested. "If we close, they might not ever come back."

Suddenly, after years of peace, we were back to arguing every day about KOB. You would have thought I'd gone behind his back and blown the roof off myself. But like it or not, KOB was coming back to our house. That weekend, about a dozen boys rolled dollies over to the center and hauled every last cabinet, computer, and printer back to my house. We spent hours pulling tacks out of walls and stacking pictures, news clippings, and awards carefully into a pile. The music studio, the art supplies, everything was loaded up.

No way was all that fitting in my house. Most of it, especially the cabinets full of papers and whatnot, went straight to the basement. I didn't move out any of my furniture, set up a mentoring space, or clear out an area for computers and printers. In my mind, this was all temporary. I just let it flow. If it bothered the kids, nobody showed it. They all sat at my big dining room table, and if somebody wanted to do homework, I brought out a computer.

It was like traveling back in time. We couldn't do art projects or put on plays anymore. Even the music studio didn't fit. I had to partner with another organization down the street who let my kids use their studio. In my house, we were down to mentoring and homework. Anybody who walked in off the street probably thought we were some kind of low-budget operation.

And yet the kids were grinning like somebody had just cooked their favorite food. They were happy to be back in my house. There was something about being in the same place where I ate my meals and slept at night that made them feel safe and comforted. They didn't care that we were all on top of each other again.

"Don't get too comfortable," I warned them. "We ain't gonna be here long. We gonna find a new building."

But it didn't quite work out that way. Month after month, there was still no building. Eventually, the Salvation Army let me use two rooms for a technology entrepreneurship program and let us play basketball on their court in the winter. It wasn't much. It wasn't what I wanted to do for the kids. But it was enough.

Months later, we were still in my house. Still down to mentoring, homework, and basketball. Still meeting around my dining room table, now well-worn with scuffs, scratches, and water rings.

I'd long since stopped telling myself we'd be out in a few weeks. I still didn't unpack all those boxes and cabinets I'd stuffed in the basement. We were doing just fine as it was, aside from the daily challenge of filling their bottomless bellies, and Lord knew I didn't have room for all that stuff anyway. Much as James fussed, I didn't mind the kids being back in my house. But sometimes, I'd look around at the kids filling every square inch of my house and think, *I could be doing so much more for them.*

My house was filled to bursting one day when my phone rang. I had to holler for everybody to hush and then duck into a corner bedroom just to hear who was on the other end.

"Is this Diane Latiker?" I heard a woman say.

"It is."

"Diane, my name is Laura. Congratulations, you've been chosen as a top-thirty finalist for the L'Oréal Woman of Worth."

I screamed so loud it's a wonder a dozen kids didn't come rushing in to save me. "Really? Oh my gosh, this is so cool!" I gushed. "Thank you, thank you, thank you!" I went on and on for at least two minutes. Poor Laura must have thought, *This lady won't let me get a word in!*

Laura told me the thirty finalists would be narrowed down to the top-ten honorees in the next few weeks. "Stay tuned," she told me. "We'll be in touch."

It was the last call I'd expected to get that day, even though I was very familiar with the Woman of Worth honor. The truth was, I'd nominated myself. A Facebook ad came across my feed one day and caught my eye. L'Oréal had been big in my house when I was growing up. If we washed our faces or smeared cream on our skin, it had to be L'Oréal.

The ad came up again and again. Something about it just stuck with me. I couldn't get it out of my head. The award was meant to honor women who ran nonprofits. Anybody who was chosen for the top ten would get $10,000 and a trip to New York for the award ceremony. But it wasn't just about the award or even the recognition it could bring KOB. My eyes were stuck on the words I'd heard repeated on L'Oréal commercials for so long: "You're worth it."

*What if they chose me?* I thought. *How amazing would it be if L'Oréal thought I was worth it?*

It was more than a slogan to me. As a black woman, I don't feel like I'm worth it in the eyes of the world most of the time. I feel like I'm in the corner, screaming at the top of my lungs,

"Hey, I'm over here! Can I at least be heard for a minute?" But in a white world, it feels like nobody hears. As I've gotten older, I've only become more invisible. My mama raised me to go for it anyway, to believe that I can do anything. And I always have.

I applied to be a L'Oréal Woman of Worth in spite of my belief that the color of my skin put me at a distinct disadvantage. That's based on a lifetime of disappointments and rejections. Like the time I drove two hours to a job interview, and because I was one minute late, the white woman who had greeted me promptly turned me away without asking me a single question. And the time a white supervisor on a construction site fired me for stopping to use the bathroom after holding it for more than three hours. I knew both situations would have had different endings if I had been white. And yet what could I do? I'd be dismissed as an angry black woman if I fought back. So I kept my head down and moved on. I bit my tongue. I held back a piece of who I really was. I kept living in this skin, even though it felt oppressive.

I thought my application would be dismissed out of hand like everything else. I dared to hope when I saw other black women had been honored in the past. Still, I was shocked when Laura called. And when she called a few weeks later to tell me I was in the top ten, I was so geeked I could have flown to New York myself. I didn't need an airplane. I was already flying high. *I'm worth it*, I thought.

My friend Lehia joined me on the trip to New York. She's handled my public relations for years—in fact, she was the one who got me my first news article when she worked in marketing for Chicago Community Trust.

A driver waited for us at the airport, holding up a sign with my name on it. He whisked us to the Quin Hotel, where all the honorees were treated to a reception. I nibbled on appetizers, taking in the plush carpet and glittering chandeliers as I met some of the most incredible women I'd ever encountered. Women who helped children stricken with cancer and disease. Women who opened their lives to young girls struggling with health issues. Women who walked across the country to raise awareness and money for asthma and bronchitis. The fact that I was being honored right alongside them felt unreal.

I woke up early the next morning for a meet and greet at the L'Oréal headquarters. We pulled up in front of the huge, shiny building, and my jaw dropped. I'd never seen anything so gorgeous. After passing through a security outfit that reminded me of the Secret Service, we took pictures with the L'Oréal president and other staffers dressed in power suits and dresses. Then, all the honorees were taken to the Bloomberg Media Group headquarters.

When I applied for the award, I didn't know it came with a day of intensive training for nonprofit leaders at Bloomberg. I wasn't exactly looking forward to it. I'd been running KOB for thirteen years and felt like I could teach my own class about what you should and shouldn't do.

I didn't have high expectations. We sat down at round tables, and a bunch of executive-types filed into the room. I prepared myself to feel bored all day. But to my surprise, this training rocked my world. My hand cramped as I scribbled notes furiously, trying to keep up.

The speakers told us we needed to think of our nonprofits not as charities but as businesses. We needed to stop thinking that we were sacrificing our lives for some noble cause. When you care about something, it isn't a sacrifice, they told us.

A man named Dave Pitts told us to stop begging people to help our nonprofits keep going. We needed to flip the script and ask them to invest in our business, because their investment will pay off. Instead of focusing on just the dire consequences of failing to help, we should paint a picture of hope and tell our investors about our specific, concrete goals.

*Oh my gosh, I've been doing this all wrong*, I thought over and over. All this time, I'd been out there telling people to help me keep kids off the street or that this fifteen-year-old has already been to jail, and he's going to go back if we don't do something. I focused on emotion, not specifics. For better or worse, people who donate to a cause want to see results. They want to see people who will go on to excel, not victims of a lost cause. They want to see a vision of hope.

Something clicked. The day I'd dreaded became a complete game changer. I knew this was why God brought me to New York. I knew this was the reason I was chosen for the Woman of Worth honor.

The award ceremony was incredible, and I teared up and laughed through the whole night. But, to be honest, I was dying to get back. I could not wait to jump back into KOB and put everything I had just learned to use. I was ready to restructure everything. I was ready to sit down with kids like Devonté and talk about his future. I was ready to change the conversation from how we keep him out of trouble to what college he wants to go to and what steps we need to take to get him there. I'd talk to him about financial aid, potential majors, and whether he'd rather live on or off campus. No more dealing in hypotheticals—I would tell the kids not only were these dreams possible, they were absolutely going to happen.

Keeping kids out of gangs wasn't enough. KOB had to become a holistic community where we dealt with every aspect of a kid's life. From the moment a kid came to us in eighth grade, we had to focus them on their future and what they wanted in life. KOB wasn't about gang members. It was about kids who might have made a wrong decision but still had a future.

I seriously upped my mentoring game too. When kids sat around my dining room table, we didn't just vent about this or that problem anymore. We talked about their dreams and goals right along with the bad. I brought in more volunteers to give more kids the opportunity to have one-on-one mentoring. Aisha stepped in to help, along with Zeek, DaJuan, Jordan, and other KOB alumni. I felt like a proud mama. I watched these kids, who had poured out their problems to me a decade ago, giving advice to younger kids now. Boys who had once sold drugs on street corners, who had carried guns in their backpacks, were now helping the next generation make better choices.

That right there is how you decrease violence. You give a kid hope. You point them toward the future. And you give them tools to get there.

*This works*, I thought. *It really works.*

# CHAPTER NINETEEN

# Fierce Over 40

I shivered backstage. I could hear the crowd screaming just beyond the curtain. I gulped. I've spoken in front of crowds before. But 250,000? That was a little more than I'd bargained for. It was certainly more than my friend Jackie had told me to expect.

Jackie had called me shortly after the 2016 presidential election, when groups across the country were scrambling to organize women's marches not just in Washington, DC, but everywhere. I'd heard Chicago was hosting one, too, and Jackie was one of the cofounders.

"How would you like to speak at the Women's March?" she asked me.

By now, I was speaking anywhere and everywhere that would let me in front of a microphone. I wanted to spread my message about helping young people and encourage everybody to care about them and invest in their futures. The first time I ever spoke at the African American Legacy Initiative in 2004, I was terrified. It was only a few dozen people, but it might as well have been a few thousand. My knees were knocking the whole time, I was stammering and sweating. But the Lord got me through. And He kept bringing me more opportunities. Every time, I felt a little more confident. Eventually, I forgot to be nervous.

At first, I'd write out every single word before I gave a speech. But every time, without fail, my heart told me to say something else. I spoke what the Lord brought to my mind. As I spoke, I could see people nodding and leaning forward, hanging on every word. So from then on, I spoke from my heart. I didn't try to impress anyone. I just spoke my truth, with no regrets. And the speaking invitations kept coming. I even spoke before the Hugh O'Brian Youth Leadership World Leadership Congress at the Superdome.

So when Jackie had told me to expect 25,000 people at the Chicago Women's March, I didn't give it a second thought. She told me I could speak about what I did with kids in Chicago and encourage other people to step up and help. The day came, and I was hopped up with energy. I couldn't wait to jump onstage and speak to thousands of women hungry for change, ready to make a difference.

James drove me downtown to Grant Park, and I lined up backstage with what felt like a gazillion other speakers. Over the course of three hours, each of us would get a few minutes to speak. I could tell the organizers were going out-of-their-minds crazy. It turned out their estimation of 25,000 people was a little off. By their count, about 250,000 people had braved the freezing temperatures and nightmarish traffic to stand through three hours of speeches. There were so many people that there wasn't even room to march. This was bigger than the Superdome. Probably bigger than any crowd I'd ever see in my lifetime. And now, all these people were about to hear about KOB.

When the emcee announced my name, she accidentally called me the lead singer of Kids Off the Block, but I was too consumed by the crowd to notice. I walked onstage and took in the sea of people stretching before me. I couldn't see the end of it. Old women and young girls. Mamas and babies in strollers. Black, white, Latina, and Asian. Well-to-do and poor. Everybody was scrunched together in their coats and pink hats. They held up signs and cheered. I drank it in, a lump forming in my throat. *These people really care*, I thought. *No way they'd be out here in the middle of this crowd if they didn't. If I could get this many people to care about helping young people, what could we do?*

I have never experienced the kind of high I did that day, shouting into the microphone as the crowd screamed and hollered.

"You might not know who I am, but I'm gonna tell you who I am." I could barely hear my own voice over the constant roar of the giant crowd. "I'm one of the thousands of women across this country who came out of their house and opened their door to the young people in their community to stop the violence." I told them my story of opening my home to gang members, troubled youth, and kids nobody else wanted to help and how I did it with no money or help, just a passion for the community.

The more they cheered, the more pumped up I got. My voice rose and I lifted my arms, my long, black peacoat flapping in the wind behind me. "I want you to care!" I shouted as the audience's cheers grew louder. "Don't forget about our young people in these neighborhoods! They need you!"

That high didn't fade as I walked off the stage and down the steps in the back. I wanted to jump in the air, pump my fist, and scream, "Yes!" I only came back to earth when I realized I had to get home somehow. James was supposed to meet me downtown, but one look at that crowd and I knew that wasn't happening. I called him and told him to meet me four blocks away, where traffic would be at least a little more manageable. Getting there, however, would be no easy task. One step at a time, I had to cross that crowd.

There was no politely sidestepping people without bumping into anybody or saying "excuse me" every time I had to squeeze past somebody. Not when everybody was standing shoulder-to-shoulder, facing the opposite direction. This was taking forever. I imagined James sitting in the car, fussing to himself as he looked at the clock.

As I walked by, a look of recognition crossed women's faces. They realized I was the same woman they'd just seen shouting at the crowd on the stage. And over and over again, they grabbed my arm to stop me. They were all the colors of the rainbow with just one thing in common—they were older women.

"I want to do something too," women said over and over. "I'm tired of being mad behind my computer. I want to do more."

They were all repeating the same refrain. One woman literally wouldn't let go of my arm.

After I finally made it out of the crowd and was back in the car with James, their words echoed in my memory. I barely answered him when he asked me how it went. My mind was in another place. I couldn't stop thinking about all these women, desperate to do something, with no idea how to break out of their everyday lives and do it.

For the last thirteen years, I had been laser-focused on young people. I woke up thinking about what somebody needed or what I could do to help them that day. I stayed up at night looking up articles on my iPad and researching ways I could run the best program. I learned their raps, ate their food, spoke their slang. I'd never looked around and thought about anybody else who could use my help. For the first time, my mind was on women my age. Women like me. Women who felt like I had thirteen years ago. They were supposed to do something, but they had no idea how to do it.

Those women at the march that day were strangers, but somehow I knew them. I was them. I knew what it was like to feel stuck in the everyday routine of dinner and dishes, house chores and homework help. As women, we put our husbands, children, even our houses before ourselves. To step out, to add one more thing to your plate, to inconvenience your family, to change the routine—it all seems scary.

Once you hit forty, it's easy to feel like your best days are over. Your kids grow up and move on, your once-crazy house is suddenly quiet and empty. You think you're too old to dream anymore, that your days stretch out before you with no excitement, no variety. If your career isn't what you'd wanted, it feels too late to make a change.

Back when my mom first told me to do something about these kids, I was so angry about the violence and hopelessness in my neighborhood. But, while I was standing by my living room window, I heard God speak so clearly it was like He was standing in the room with me. He wanted me to walk outside and bring those kids into my home. I had nothing more than my living room and an itty-bitty laptop to research after-school programs. I had no experience. I wasn't qualified. I had to learn and make mistakes along the way. Now I have a life because of KOB. I still have my family. I still love taking care of them, and being a wife and mother is still my top priority. But I have a life that doesn't depend on them. And that makes me jump out of bed in the morning ready to go. I don't live with regrets. I don't lie in bed thinking I should have or I could have. I did. Because the Lord called me to do it.

Would I have had the courage to follow the Lord's call if my mom hadn't pushed and prodded me along? She called out the Lord's anointing on me. She brought it up every chance she got and wouldn't let me off the hook. If I hadn't listened to God, I would have had to face my mama.

*What if these women had somebody mentoring them?* I thought. What if somebody helped them figure out their passion? What if someone just pushed them in the right direction? What if they understood they could get going with no degree or special training and that nobody was holding them back but themselves? If I could do it, then surely they could too.

I couldn't get the thought out of my head. I lay in bed that night, trying to go to sleep. This new idea was there when I dragged myself out of bed the next morning and planned what the kids and I would do that evening. I felt just like I had back when I was first starting KOB. And I'd learned enough by then to know that when a thought won't leave my head, it's from the Lord. And if it's from the Lord, I'd better listen.

Suddenly, it came to me. I picked up the phone and called Jackie and Lehia. "We gotta do something to help women get involved. I want to call it Fierce Over 40."

The vision was so clear now. I saw us creating a mentoring program for women in their forties, fifties, sixties, seventies, and beyond. We'd set up a website, send out newsletters, and host events to help encourage women to stop writing angry posts on Facebook, get out from behind their computers, and go do something. Wherever they may be, with whatever tools or abilities they may have, we'd encourage them to go do something.

Jackie and Lehia sat down with me and helped me write out a plan for this new undertaking. Then, when I told one of my friends about the idea, she had the idea to launch it at the Black Women's Expo. She brought me straight to the founder, and, oh boy, we were off and running.

Dozens of women stopped by our booth to sign up for our newsletter and mentoring events. Just like at the Women's March, I heard again and again about how they desperately wanted to do something but didn't know how to get started. I told them I wasn't just offering them a website and an email address. I gave them my home address. I told them to stop by anytime and I'd help them face-to-face.

It was just like KOB. When you open up your door with the Lord's blessing, the people will come. People like Denise Richards—not the actress. She was a nurse who worked in a hospital taking care of babies. She sat in my living room one day crying her eyes out.

"I just want to do something," she said. "I love babies, and they're dying."

She told me she was sick of seeing babies writhing in pain from diseases that were completely preventable. She hated watching mothers deliver unhealthy babies because they either didn't have access to prenatal care or just didn't come to their appointments. She felt helpless standing by, watching it all happen, unable to stop it.

"So, you're in the facility with them?" I asked her. "What's holding you back from doing something?"

Denise confided that the hospital has rules about what nurses can and can't do. If she passed out pamphlets or gave advice that didn't come from the hospital, she could find herself out on the street and out of a job.

I understood where she was coming from. I remembered what it was like to bend over backward to keep a job. But I also thought her words sounded a lot like an excuse.

I sat next to her and put my arm around her shoulders. "You have the whole world at your fingertips," I told her. "You have a computer. Why don't you start a website? Just one page. Then see what else you feel like you can do."

She nodded slowly. I could see the wheels turning in her mind.

"Then you reach out," I said. "Show your website to your friends and family. Let people know you have it. See if they're interested in helping you. Because you probably got other nurses and doctors who care about this same issue. You're not alone out there."

Denise listened. She walked out my door determined to make a difference. I kept meeting with her regularly as she started a website and created one-pagers of information on infant and maternal health care. She created a group of like-minded people to help her research and brainstorm ideas. And she's well on her way to creating a 501(c)(3) nonprofit. She's not crying anymore. She's empowered. Fierce Over 40 did that.

Helping women like Denise spurred a new passion inside me. I had no idea that other women were like me, afraid to step out from the sidelines. They just needed somebody to say, "You can do it." Women came to me who were divorced, widowed, single, empty nesters, searching for that thing in their life that lights their heart on fire. Some of them had given up on their dreams when they were younger. Some of them truly believed that life had passed them by. I told them that it's not too late. They're not trapped. They're free.

I felt inspired and energized seeing other women realize that maybe, just maybe, they had dreams left to dream. They could go volunteer at a homeless shelter or start one themselves if one didn't exist in their area. They could create a website, mentor a kid, visit the elderly. Wherever they were, whatever resources they had, there was something they could do to make a difference.

My energy and excitement must have been contagious, because it wasn't long before Aisha approached me. "Ma, what about young women?" she asked. "We want to do something too."

I don't know if I'd ever been prouder than I was in that moment. I grinned and wrapped my arms around her in a big bear hug. "Let's do something about that."

Together we created a sister organization, Fierce Under 40. Aisha volunteered to be the president and to help mentor women who came to her.

*Aisha sure grew up to be something*, I thought, my heart about to burst. A tall, intelligent, strong woman stood where a gangly girl once had. In Aisha, I saw the past and the future of KOB. One day, I'll be too old to run around after these teenagers. When that day comes, I know Aisha will be ready to take the reins. Lord knows she could run this program in her sleep already.

I started Fierce Over 40 for other women, but it turned out the Lord wasn't done giving me dreams. The more I mentored other women, the more the Lord spoke to my heart. Opening up my front door was just the first step, He showed me. There are kids who need help in other cities too. Kids who aren't welcome at other organizations. Kids who just need somebody to give them goals for the future, to speak hope into their lives, to show them that there's more available to them than drugs and gangs. I've seen them myself when I've traveled around the country on a bus, showing the kids in KOB that there's more to the world than their little neighborhood.

*More cities need KOB*, I clearly felt the Lord tell me. People who are fed up with violence in their communities need someone to help them open their own grassroots programs and mentor kids on their blocks. I started to dream of traveling to cities and helping to raise up people in their neighborhoods. I could mentor them, showing them what I've learned and starting them off on the right foot.

I'm no expert. I've done what I could by the grace of God. I'm certainly not qualified to teach people how to open a nonprofit. But if the Lord has called me, then I know He'll equip me for the job. He's never let me down yet.

# Look What God Did

Every neighborhood has that building that seems like it's got a new business every week. In Roseland, it was a brown brick building next to the Houston and Gale towers that once upon a time was a grocery store as well as a barber shop, then an airbrush shop that made our T-shirts and wrote names on stones for the memorial. Back in 1988, when James and I moved onto Michigan, everybody stopped at that grocery store for chips and hot sauce and snacks. Then the owner added a liquor store. But that only lasted until the new congressman, who'd made it his mission to take the liquor stores off corners, shut it down.

The owner was not one to be discouraged. Before you knew it, the building was up and running again as a barbecue joint that pumped out the mouth-watering scent of ribs and brisket every single day. Eventually, that restaurant closed down, and a catering business moved in. That lasted about two years before it closed for good. After that, the space sat empty.

I'd had my eye on that building for at least ten years. Every time I saw the owner, I asked him how much he'd let it go for. Every time, he gave me a different answer. He started at $130,000—way out of my range. After the recession hit in 2008, he dropped it down to $90,000, and then $86,500. When he finally went down to $80,000, I got excited. It wasn't like I could go out and buy that building the next day, but it was doable. We could raise that kind of money one day, I thought.

God just wouldn't take that building off my heart. Every time a donor came to visit or I got a big-name guest, I walked them over to the building. "One day, I believe God is going to give KOB this building," I told them. Everybody promised to help. Most people didn't follow through. But I didn't stop believing. I knew my mom prayed on it. She even walked around the whole building with her anointing oil, knocking on heaven's door.

For a while, I rented the empty space in that building. That had been the center, KOB's home, until the roof caved in. And even though the landlord never did fix that roof, I didn't give up on that building. All it needed was some love. I just knew we could buy it and fix it up and use all that space to revolutionize the neighborhood. If I thought we were doing great things just in my living room, there was no telling what we could do with a place like that.

God had given me a burning desire to open up a technology entrepreneurship center. I envisioned young people working with professionals to learn everything from coding to graphic design. I wanted them to learn how to make solar panels. I wanted to provide training for skilled trades like construction, plumbing, and carpentry. The whole place would be state-of-the-art and staffed with only the best teachers. Any kid who went through the program would leave with the skills to get a job and make great money. And, of course, we'd have a music studio so the young people could have an artistic outlet.

I've been working with young people long enough to know that the number-one factor leading to violence is hopelessness. Kids who see no path for themselves beyond the gangs, who see drug dealing as their most likely profession, who don't have a prayer of getting into college, much less paying for it—these are the kids who think they're worthless. In their eyes, their lives are disposable. When they have nothing to lose, they're not afraid to take risks. Risks like carrying a gun in their backpack and shooting somebody who looks at them wrong or who says the wrong thing. A kid with nothing to lose is dangerous.

If these kids had skills, if they were employable, if they could make a big, fat paycheck, it would change the game completely. They would have something to live for. Something to lose. I truly believe that violence wouldn't be an issue if kids had the right training and could get good jobs. I can't redevelop my neighborhood myself or convince city officials to bring businesses, jobs, and places of entertainment to Roseland. Those investments would make a huge difference, but I also understand a violent neighborhood is a tough sell to a major corporation. I couldn't change our circumstances, but I could equip kids to get jobs and make better lives for themselves.

I just couldn't do it in my living room. I needed more room. And that would require a true act of God. *Lord, we need a miracle*, I prayed over and over.

I truly believed that God would give the building to us in His time. But my mom also taught me that God doesn't want us to sit on our hands doing nothing. So I talked about the building every chance I got—including during my speech at the L'Oréal Woman of Worth awards. As I spoke of my dreams for the future, I told the crowd about the building on my street that I had set my sights on and what we could do if only we could buy it.

Now, I knew there were celebrities in the audience. I knew that supermodel Karlie Kloss was watching. I'd shouted hello to her as I was in the middle of taking a picture with Diane Keaton. But I honestly never thought twice about what they might do once they returned home.

A few weeks after the ceremony, though, I was back in my house, scrolling through Facebook, when I saw I had a new notification. Somebody had tagged me in a video. That somebody was Karlie Kloss. My whole body went numb as I saw the video had over two thousand likes. *That can't be right*, I thought.

But it was. There was Karlie, as beautiful as always, telling the entire internet that she was "left speechless" by my story and asking people to donate and help me buy the building. Tears rolled down my face as I listened to her talk about how I inspired her with my work and my passion and how she wanted to help.

*Nobody's really going to donate*, I thought. *Who would give money to some stranger they don't know nothing about?*

But I was wrong. The next thing I knew, Karlie's people contacted me to set up a way that people could donate directly to my building fund. And the money just poured in. Every time I checked the bank account, there was more. I was living in a dream, in complete euphoria. *We're going to get that building*, I thought. I'd hoped and prayed for so long. I'd believed in my heart that God would give it to me. But I'm only human. I'd be lying if I said I didn't ever think, *Dang, I'm not going to get it*. Now, it was on the cusp of happening, and He was the only One who could get credit for it. Why else would an international supermodel plead my case to the world?

Within a week and a half, people I'd never even laid eyes on had donated over $55,000. I was in complete disbelief. In ten years, I hadn't raised a fraction of that amount. The money from *Secret Millionaire* and my CNN Hero award was long gone by now, after replacing a van, paying rent on our old building space, and keeping these kids fed and clothed. But now we were more than halfway to $80,000.

*Ain't that just like God?* I thought. It was a beautiful feeling, to feel so supported by God and the people who cared about His vision for helping kids. I wanted to make sure He got the glory. This was beyond me. Beyond any human. I took out my phone and recorded a video to post to Facebook thanking every single person who had given a few dollars and telling them about our hopes for the building.

I knew $55,000 wasn't the amount the building owner had told me, but I figured it was worth a shot. I called him up and told him how much we'd raised. "Would you consider selling it for that amount?" I asked him.

God has worked plenty of miracles in my life, but this was one instance where He chose not to move. "I'm already letting it go at a bargain," the owner said flatly.

I hung up the phone feeling discouraged. I'd felt such a high seeing all those donations pour in. I thought for sure we were *this close* to getting a building. All those people who gave me money were counting on us buying it. But now, I had no idea how we'd come up with the rest of the cash.

I had one last thought. One Hail Mary. Maybe L'Oréal could help. They believed in KOB. They knew how important our work was. Maybe they would stand in the gap.

So I wrote an email. I told L'Oréal all about Karlie and the video, about how much money had poured in and how much we still had left to go. I sent them Karlie's video. And I prayed as I hit Send. *It's in God's hands now. He got us this far. He's not going to leave us hanging now.*

And He didn't. My heart about burst out of my chest when I read L'Oréal's response saying they'd see what they could do to help. Don't ask me what strings they pulled or who they had to convince to say yes. But it wasn't long before they called to tell me they'd cover the rest of the money I needed for the building.

*Thank you, Jesus*, I prayed over and over.

The day I closed on the building, my whole family gathered in my backyard to celebrate. We barbecued rib tips for everybody—Aisha and her new fiancé, my mom, James, my auntie, my daughters, my grandsons. Music blared from a speaker as we laughed together, releasing the tension we'd felt waiting for this building.

I couldn't keep my eyes off my mom. Her face had a few more lines since the day she'd told me I should do something with those kids all those years before, her hair was a little grayer. But the light in her eyes never changed. The light that came from her devotion to the Lord, her constant belief that He would show up and do what He had said He'd do.

"I knew God was gonna do it," she said, smiling as she shook her head. "I just knew it. When you pray to God, you just got to wait on Him. It's on His time. And He did it."

But we weren't done waiting on God. We still aren't. We bought that building knowing it's nothing but a shell. It needs walls. New flooring. Heating and air conditioning. A new roof—that landlord never did fix it when it fell in years before. One contractor estimated it would cost $55,000 to fix it up, and that was on the low end.

I look around that building now and see the missing walls, the dirty floor, even a toilet and sink sitting in the middle of a room, disconnected from any kind of plumbing. Anybody else might look at this building and think it's hopeless. But I know better than that. I'm not worried. I don't know how we're going to raise the money, but it doesn't keep me up at night. I know God is going to do it. Fixing up a building isn't too hard for Him. He's come through every step of the way. He's accomplished the impossible many times before.

Take James. Back in 2003, he walked around our house grumbling and fussing about these kids taking over his castle. I laugh when I tell the story of the TV now, but it sure wasn't funny then. For a while, I really wondered if he might divorce me over Kids Off the Block. But God came through. He changed his heart. Now James is my partner, my biggest supporter next to my mom. When I look at the building, he's right there with me, nodding his head and saying, "God's gonna do it. Don't even worry about it."

Or my daughter Aisha. She was just thirteen years old when I flipped our lives upside down, inviting all her friends into our house. She didn't want to share her mama then. She wasn't sure if I had enough love in my heart to go around. But I did. And I do. I know KOB has transformed her into the confident, take-charge woman she is today. I know she's the future of KOB, and I know God will equip her just like He equipped me.

I look at kids like Zeek. That boy had the worst attitude in the South Side when he walked in my door, with those big lips of his sticking out so far it would have been funny if it hadn't made me so mad. He sure wasn't somebody I would tell other kids to look up to. And now here he is, mentoring kids, writing positive raps, and helping me at programming.

I point to kids like Darrell, the boy who lived next door with his brother, Levi. He was quiet and withdrawn when my little music studio drew him over to my house and into KOB. At twenty-six years old the last time he came to see me, you couldn't shut him up. He's the top salesperson at his job, he has a beautiful fiancée, and he's got two adorable children. When he saw me, he wrapped me up in a big bear hug.

"Miss Diane, I was desensitized to everything going on, but you helped me," he told me. "Thank you for giving me confidence."

I've got a whole list of kids who earned scholarships to colleges in Illinois and Wisconsin. Kids who got their high school diplomas when everybody said they'd drop out. It seems like a week doesn't go by without somebody stopping by my house or sending me a message on social media to tell me how KOB changed their lives.

Sometimes you don't see it right away. The thing about helping kids is that it's messy. You can show them a better way, but you can't change their circumstances. You can't take them away from the gang on their block or the cousin who's a bad influence or their family history of dealing drugs. So sometimes, a lot of times, they fall. They mess up. Maybe they don't drop out of their gang right away, maybe they keep selling drugs, but you don't give up. You keep planting the seed, not knowing when it will finally grow. Their lives are still worth saving, no matter how many mistakes they make. You just never know if this is the time it will sink in.

And sometimes success is just keeping their names out of my memorial. Just keeping them alive is a victory. Especially when they seem hell-bent on putting themselves in situations that land them staring down the barrel of a gun.

It's not for the faint of heart or the easily discouraged. Too many mornings, I've opened my eyes and thought, *I can't do this anymore. I can't take the heartbreak one more second.* Like the morning after TO was killed. Mornings after stepping between two boys pointing pistols at one another. Mornings after finding a mama sobbing at the memorial, clutching a stone with her baby's name on it. It hurts. It never stops, even after all these years.

And yet, I'm still here. By God's grace, I keep going. He pushes me forward, gives me strength, guides my steps. He's the reason this started in the first place. He's the reason we're still going, still reaching new kids every day. He's the reason teenage boys still want to hang out with an old lady with no money and no training.

People sometimes ask me if I ever look back in amazement at what I've done. How I started with a handful of kids in my living room and ended up running a flow-blown program. How I've saved lives, turned kids around, cut the violence in my neighborhood. Honestly, I don't want to look back. I'm afraid that will trick me into thinking I did this, that it will give me some kind of glory. I don't want that. God needs every bit of the glory. He deserves it. Make no mistake, this isn't about me. I'm not special. God didn't pick me because I'm talented or knowledgeable. He used me because I said yes. I followed Him out of my house and out of my comfort zone. And He does the same for anybody who follows Him.

I don't know how God's going to get us enough money to fix up this new building, but I know He'll find a way. I'm not intimidated anymore. My faith makes me believe in things beyond me. Fixing up this building is beyond me. But so was inviting a few kids into my living room. All God wants us to do is answer His call. We don't have to figure it out. God's got it.

Anybody can make a difference right where they are with whatever they have. You don't need money or education or even a plan. You just need to follow God. Listen to His call. Care about His people. His children. And do something. Don't wait for a sign from heaven or for a check to come in the mail. Save a teen. Do something.

# Acknowledgments

Jeff Stroy worked for over a year to bring this book to life. He believed in me and the vision. Without him there wouldn't be a book. Jeff, you tirelessly pursued everyone, every lead, until you got others to believe, and for that I am forever thankful and grateful.

Wes Yoder, thank you for believing in this project and for influencing others to believe. You took the vision and made it a reality for me, my family, and the youth we serve.

Bethany Mauger, I knew when I first met you that you understood every word I wanted to say without me even saying it! I am so proud to have worked with you on this project, so proud of how you wrote my story. Thank you for giving me a voice to share with the world.

To my mom: GOD gave you a vision to give to me, and you encouraged me to fulfill it. Your words and prayers every day kept me going, your love gave me the strength to keep going. It is because of you that I found my passion and that I was able to impact the lives of so many young people. I love you, Mom, and thank you!

To my husband, James: Thank you so much for always supporting me 100 percent! I could not have done it without you; your dedication to the youth was unmatched. You fed them, mentored them, washed their clothes, and drove them around this entire city. I love you!

To my daughter Aisha: GOD made all of this possible because of and through you! You have been my ride or die, literally being by my side through the good and bad of this journey. Thank you, Baby Girl, aka Mommy. I love you always and forever!

To my sister Tammy: Thank you, Sis, for always being my number-one cheerleader, telling everyone you meet about your sister and advocating on my behalf. I love you sincerely, and I'm so grateful for your support!

To my sister-in-law Lillian: Thank you for being there when I needed you the most, for loving the youth with all your heart, and for advocating on their behalf. I am so blessed to have you by my side. I love you!

Special thanks to all the donors, volunteers, and mentors who have guided me, funded KOB, and helped where needed. I appreciate you all!

To all the young people: Thank you for allowing me to be in your lives, to listen to your stories and concerns. Also, thank you for inspiring me to do more and for giving me an opportunity to help in some small way. I love you!

**Diane Latiker** was a Top 10 CNN Hero of the Year in 2011 for her tireless work with at-risk Chicago teens. Recipient of a 2013 BET Shine a Light Award, she is an in-demand speaker and has been featured by national media outlets such as NBC News, CBS News, NPR's *Weekend Edition*, *Ebony* magazine, *Time* magazine, the *Huffington Post*, *USA Today*, and more. In 2019, she spoke at the US House Judiciary Committee's first hearing on gun violence in years and has just graduated from the Goldin Institute as a 2019 Chicago Peace Fellow. Latiker lives in Chicago.

**Bethany Mauger** is the coauthor of *Free Cyntoia: My Search for Redemption in the American Prison System*, as well as an award-winning journalist who has spent more than a decade writing about everything from the Great Recession to inspiring stories of people making a difference. Recognized by the Hoosier State Press Association for her local coverage of various issues ranging from the economy to community service, Mauger lives in Lansing, Michigan, with her husband and two young sons.

# Connect with Diane

diane.latiker

dianekob

latikerdiane

Interested in booking Diane for a

**speaking engagement?**

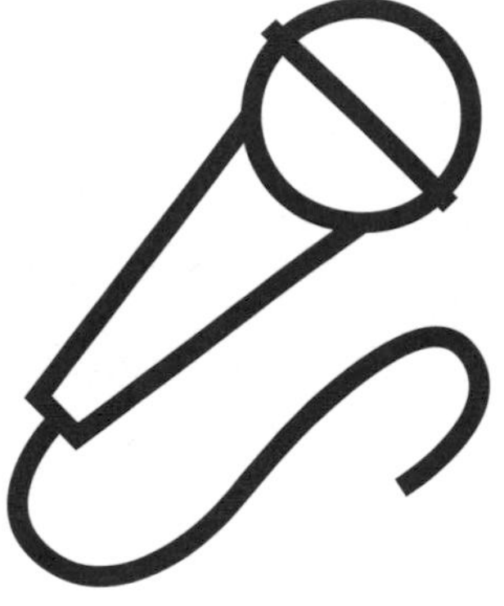

Contact her at

**diane.latiker@gmail.com**

# Awards

Diane was a CNN **Top 10 Hero of the Year** in 2011, a recipient of the 2013 BET **Shine a Light** Award, and a L'Oréal Paris USA "Women of Worth" **Top 10 Honoree** in 2016.

CNN HEROES

## Stay CONNECTED with

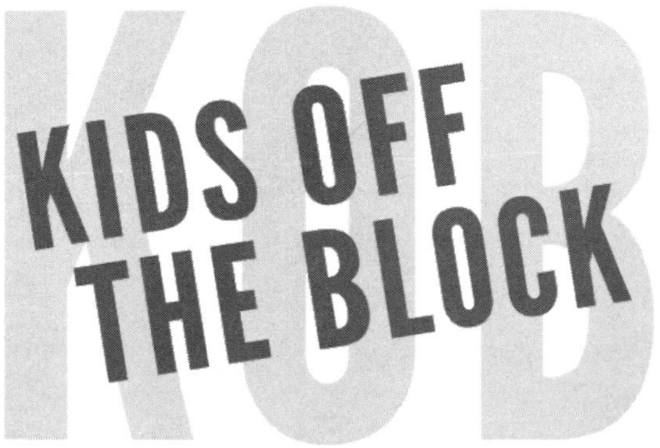


To stay up to date with what's going on with Kids Off the Block, to donate, or to contact them, head to

**KIDSOFFTHEBLOCK.US**

---

**Or follow them on social media!**